FATAL OR FRAGILE

FATAL OR FRAGILE

WENDY VARGA

WENDY VARGA
MINISTRIES

FriesenPress

Suite 300 - 990 Fort St
Victoria, BC, V8V 3K2
Canada

www.friesenpress.com

First Edition — 2019

ISBN
978-1-5255-4682-2 (Hardcover)
978-1-5255-4683-9 (Paperback)
978-1-5255-4684-6 (eBook)

1. RELIGION, CHRISTIAN LIFE, SPIRITUAL WARFARE

Distributed to the trade by The Ingram Book Company

Dedication

I dedicate this book to anyone entangled in satan's sinister plot—escape is possible!

Dear Reader

All is not lost! What you thought was the end is only the beginning! You are far more powerful than you think. Discover how to sweep satan's intricate death trap away to nothingness!

Endorsements

Reading Wendy's book brought back recollections of my unique, personal experience of being stung by a scorpion while staying in a Nicaraguan home. Wendy has painted a vivid picture of the supernatural battle we're in. Packed with multiple layers of spiritual lessons, *Fatal or Fragile* will enrich even the most mature believer. Written for those who seriously desire to walk in a higher level of spiritual maturity.

—Martin Mann
CEO/Pastor of Jitters Coffee House
a market-place ministry

A panoramic view of the forces working against us, their tactics, and our futile attempts at overcoming them on our own, this book is a description of the ultimate price that was paid. Wendy depicts this truth in a fresh new way that captivates the reader and infuses with life, hope, and trust.

—George Woodward
Canadian Reformation Director

You can never win a raging war without knowing the enemy's tactics and having a specific battle plan. *Fatal or Fragile* is a powerful, revelatory book that gives keys on how you can escape the fatality of the enemy's death grip. Come and explore the mystery of how to be an overcomer!

—Pastors Moses & Rosemary Sabo
Portal of Glory Christian Ministries Int'l

Note from the Editor

The reality of spiritual warfare, viewed by many as an abstract, "other dimension" concept, is literally "brought down to earth" in Wendy Varga's unique analogical book, *Fatal or Fragile.* Comparing Satan's wiles and attacks to the physiology and activities of spiders and snakes, she provides a biblical guide to withstanding demonic onslaught and tearing down the webs of the enemy. Scientifically and theologically informative, *Fatal or Fragile* will inspire believers with confidence and encourage the battle-weary in the church ... It's a brilliant combination of scripture study, etymology, biology, and theology, and it was an educational pleasure to read ... Wendy's strong writing skills and thorough research have made it an engaging and inspiring project that will be a blessing to many.

TABLE OF CONTENTS

1. THE MESSAGE OF THE WEB

The light breeze was a welcomed friend as I sat back on my seat, finally able to relax. The highway's slight incline had seemed endless and caused further strain to already exhausted muscles. From here, it was a small downhill coast into town. Sunny, warm, and delightfully beautiful, the day was perfect for a ride. Cycling to raise money for missions, we pulled up to the delegated rest stop, ready for a revitalizing drink and something to rev up our energy levels. My brother and I arrived ahead of the rest of the cyclers and walked in to see what there was for refreshment. Quickly noticing that someone had left a beautifully wrapped package of "trail mix" on the table for us, I reached for it, wondering who would have been so thoughtful and kind. Excited about the unexpected "treat," I decided to examine it more closely before ripping off the clear layer of cellophane and trying a taste. Maybe, just maybe, I would discover a clue as to who had left it for us. Elation was quickly replaced by revulsion, and excitement quickly turned to despair as I read words that at first were almost imperceptible but became blatantly obvious after first notice: witchcraft occult satanism. Not wanting anyone to taste or even touch the "treat," I quickly put it away in a safe place.

Shaken and shocked … I awoke from my sleep!

Needless to say, my morning began with much contemplation. A continual repeat button seemed to be pressed. The dream cycled incessantly through my mind as the day got underway. Completely absorbed in my thoughts, I stopped at a drop-off point to collect some papers for work. Reaching into a ticket box hanging at eye-level, I collected the papers we needed. Instantly, my hand jerked back! A gasp of horror escaped from my lips as I caught a glimpse of something very large and very black fall in front of me. It happened so rapidly and so close to my face that it took a second for my brain to catch up. Shuddering, I knew that a very large spider had dropped right in front of me. *Spiders are symbolic of the occult* was my first thought as the words of the "trail mix" still ran rampant through my mind. My first reaction was fear and I desperately wondered, *God, what is going on? How can this be when I've applied your blood?*

His response was immediate. *What happened?*

It fell right in front of me! I replied (as if He didn't know).

Yes, it fell! He patiently responded. *It fell right in front of your eyes! And it fell so quickly that you could hardly distinguish what it was. Just like I watched Satan fall like lightning from heaven, he fell before you so quickly that you could hardly even discern it was him. He fell before you because you're covered with the blood, and nothing shall by any means harm you.*

The Lord's gentle rebuke calmed my soul, causing the night's dream and falling spider to fade from my thoughts. The morning was beautiful, crisp, and cold. My every footstep crunched as I walked through a thick carpet of snow sparkling like diamonds in the early morning light. Tree branches sagged, drooping heavily under the weight of fresh snowfall. Invigorated, my now carefree heart delighted in the magnificence of winter's frosty morning. My steps were quicker, my breaths much deeper, and my thoughts much lighter when, suddenly, I jerked to the side to avoid something that glimmered in the dawn's early light. The sight of it jolted me out of my reverie and back to thoughts of my dream and earlier encounter with the spider.

I almost walked right into a spider's web! The words screamed through my head. I stopped to stare, shocked by the consistency of the morning's events.

A web that would normally be nearly imperceptible was now made astoundingly visible by the early morning frost. There it hung, glistening with wondrous appeal and attraction, looking nearly flawless. I was taken aback by its beauty.

What if I'd walked into this web? I berated myself. The answer soon drifted through my spirit. *Nothing! Nothing would have happened! I would've just walked right through it, and the web would have been destroyed.*

The answer soothed my soul, yet my heart now intently pondered the dream, the spider, and the web—bringing me to another question: *Is this web fatal or fragile?*

I knew there was a message in the web.

2.
THE CURSE OF THE WEB

Contemplating my new thoughts, I could barely drag myself away. The web's vibrant beauty astounded me. Silken strands sagged under the weight of winter's frost. Ice crystals made the once almost imperceptible trap astoundingly visible, showing off its beauty and resiliency. How many times had I walked into spider webs, completely unaware that they were there until I felt the uncomfortable, eerie feeling of invisible strands clinging to my face and hair? How many times had I groped in desperation at the feel of invisible threads that clung to my arms and legs while walking through fields and forest, shuddering in horror at any thought that the weaver-of-the-web may still be on me?

The weaver-of-the-web—the spider—so skilled at fabricating an almost imperceptible, intricate web. This proficient weaver has often been used to symbolically represent a higher, dark power.

> Spiders—and their webs… Tattered webbing is a feature of any horror flick, an icon of the evil that is lurking about with the spiders themselves often taking the role of vicious instruments of a higher, dark power.[1]

Ironically, Scripture also uses spiders as a symbol of demonic forces and their power. Scripture speaks about "…serpents and scorpions, and … all the power of the enemy…" (Luke 10:19). Interestingly, **scorpions belong to the spider family!**

> Scorpions were a species of spider. They abounded in the Jordan valley.[2]

Not only horror flicks, but Scripture also uses scorpions (spiders) to represent a dark power along with another representation of evil—snakes. We find references in Scripture likening satan to a snake.

…that old serpent, called the Devil, and Satan…
Revelation 12:9 **(and)*** *Revelation 20:2*

*(When God says something once, it's important, but when God says the exact same thing twice, it's like He's

1 Hawkes, Alison. *Here We Go A-Spidering.* https://baynature.org/article/spiders/

2 Staggs, Brandon. SwordSearcher, *Easton's Bible Dictionary.* iPhone app. Apple App Store. Vers. 3.4. Brandon Staggs, 1999.

placing an exclamation point or two on that particular phrase.) In the book of Revelation, we're given the name of the angel, or king of the demonic powers, from the bottomless pit.

> *...the angel from the bottomless pit; his name in Hebrew is Abaddon, and in Greek, Apollyon—**the Destroyer**.*
>
> *Revelation 9:11 (NLT)*

Ironically, the numbers of this Scripture reference are 9-1-1 (In North-America, the number 911 is reserved for emergency circumstances only). In this emergency-number reference, we're given the name of the one who is on a deadly hunt to attack and kill, the one who brings trauma, crisis, and calamity—the Destroyer. From this same bottomless pit, we see that the power given to the serpent's forces is likened to the power of scorpions (spiders).

> *When he opened the Abyss ... out of the smoke locusts came down on the earth and were given power like that of **scorpions**...*
>
> *Revelation 9:2-3 (NIV)*

Many similarities can be seen between the activity of the demonic forces and the activity of spiders. Consequently, there arises a connection between spider, occult, serpents, and curses.

> The term *occult* comes from the Latin *occultus*, which means concealed or hidden from the eyes of understanding.[3]
>
> —Ken and Jean Harrington

The objective of the occult is to manipulate and control people and situations by uncovering hidden information and using it against them. The objective of the web is also to manipulate. It controls the prey caught in it for the spider's advantage—namely, to feed the spider. An access point of demonic activity is a nearly invisible web the enemy weaves for us. His traps are often well-concealed, and the end result or consequence of his trap is hidden from our understanding. Had we known the end result, we would have stayed far, far away and been far, far more careful!

Spiders and snakes are remarkably similar. Both have poor eyesight. Both molt because their outer covering has a limited capacity for growth. Neither has a visible ear; therefore, they both "hear" by feeling vibrations. Another commonality is people's instinctive negative reaction toward them. Snakes and spiders are two of the most feared animals on the planet, and both are predatory.

3 Harrington, Ken and Jeanne. *From Curses to Blessings*, Destiny Image Publishers, Inc. Shippensburg, PA. 2011. Pg 42.

> The fear of snakes (ophiophobia or herpetophobia) is one of the most common phobias worldwide.[4]

> Spiders and scorpions are considered to be two of the most feared animals… Their behavior and habits are also somewhat similar. Both are predatory and obtain nutrition by catching and consuming other [prey]…[5]

Satan is also predatory. Like the spider, he's always seeking whom he may devour. His simple job description is to steal, kill, destroy!

> *…the devil, is on the prowl … seeking someone to devour.*
>
> *1 Peter 5:8 (CEB)*

His very objective is destruction, and YOU are his target!

The first mention of curse in Scripture is found in Genesis 3, where it's mentioned in conjunction with the serpent. The snake was cursed. In keeping with the law of first mention, we know that because of the ancient serpent—satan—the curse has come. The natural serpent in the garden wasn't satan but did allow him to use his body. Therefore, the serpent was cursed and has come to epitomize evil.

---

4 Lenhardt, Karin. *76 Interesting Facts about Snakes.* https://www.factretriever.com/snake-facts

5 *Spider vs. Scorpion Identification.* https://www.orkin.com/stinging-pests/scorpions/spider-vs-scorpion-identification/

*And the LORD God said unto the **serpent**, Because thou hast done this, thou art **cursed**...*

Genesis 3:14

In Genesis 3:14, *cursed* is the Hebrew word [arar] which means: to execrate.

> Execrate is derived from the Latin execrates: ex– meaning out, and sacrare– meaning consecrated, from the root sacer– meaning sacred. Thus the root of the verb *"to be cursed"* means *to be removed from a consecrated or sacred position.*[6]
>
> —Ken and Jean Harrington

Satan was cursed, cast down from his sacred position. Consequently, he greatly envies that we have been given a place in Christ Jesus—which is *far above* all principalities and powers (that would include him). Therefore, the very objective of satan's web is to pull us down from our consecrated, sacred position. And every web begins with a single strand.

> Every web begins with a single thread, which forms the basis of the rest of the structure. To establish this bridge, the spider climbs to a suitable starting point (up a tree branch, for example) and releases a length of thread into the wind. With any luck, the free end

6 Harrington, Ken and Jeanne. *From Curses to Blessings*, Destiny Image Publishers, Inc. Shippensburg, PA. 2011. Pg 36.

> of the thread will catch on to another branch. If the spider feels that the thread has caught onto something, it cinches up the silk and attaches the thread to the starting point.[7]

Satan releases a single strand of his web in hopes that it will latch onto you and allow him to reel you in—or, in other words, pull you down from your sacred position.

> A curse always lowers who we are.[8]
>
> —Ken and Jean Harrington

> ...the curse removes us from our exalted position in the heavenlies, our sacred place, and entangles us in satan's realm.[9]
>
> —Ken and Jean Harrington

Whenever we get entangled in satan's web, our lives instantly become increasingly and strangely complicated, and we start heading on a path that leads in a downward spiral toward death. We can fall prey to that which he has concealed simply through carelessness or ignorance, or he will expose his web in a display of powerful and mysterious

7 Harris, Tom. *How Spiders Work.* https://animals.howstuffworks.com/arachnids/spider5.htm

8 Harrington, Ken and Jeanne. *From Curses to Blessings*, Destiny Image Publishers, Inc. Shippensburg, PA. 2011. Pg 37.

9 Harrington, Ken and Jeanne. *From Curses to Blessings*, Destiny Image Publishers, Inc. Shippensburg, PA. 2011. Pg 38.

attractiveness in the hopes of luring us into his vast, satanic web tied to hell. His web, if you can see it, may look like a thing of beauty, yet it's a trap meant to be fatal.

> The spider web, I want to suggest, offers an apposite metaphor for a world that holds itself in precarious balance, that tenses itself with violence and catastrophe but also with grace and beauty, and that calls out and silhouettes promissory worlds of entanglements. However, what draws me to the metaphoric seduction of the spiderweb, I must add, is one specific trait: it's semblance and vocation as a trap. Spiderwebs are traps.[10]

Satan's web, displayed with so much grace and beauty, is tensed and full of violence and catastrophe. The violence and catastrophe (end results) are very much like the writing on our "trail mix"—nearly imperceptible at first, but blatantly obvious after first notice. The enemy's promises may look enticingly beautiful and satisfying, but the end result is a world of entanglement. It is *always* a trap!

Satan's web, displayed with so much grace and beauty, is tensed and full of violence and catastrophe.

10 Jimenez, Alberto Corsin. Spanish National Research Council, *Spider web anthropology's: ecologies, infrastructures, entanglement's*, http://digital.csic.es/bitstream/10261/134351/1/spiderweb%20anthros_160209.pdf

> In constructing a web, a spider has created an ideal trap. Delicate and transparent … yet, they are also incredibly strong and sticky…[11]

> The silk in a spider's web is five times stronger than a strand of steel that is the same thickness.[12]

The spider's web is:

> Vibrant yet fragile, interactive and responsive whilst simultaneously resilient and solicitous…[13]

Webs are resilient, strong, delicate, and fragile architecture in a strategic display!

Delicate and strong? Fragile and resilient? Vastly opposite words describing the very same trap. Resilient and strong with an *appearance* of vibrant beauty! No wonder the web has been fatal to so many. No wonder so many have been caught up in its entanglements. Webs are resilient, strong, delicate, fragile architecture in a strategic display. Silken strands with greater tensile strength than steel—a death trap to so many.

11 Hawkes, Alison. *Here We Go A-Spidering.* https://baynature.org/article/spiders/

12 Lehnardt, Karin. *84 Amazing Facts about Spiders.* https://www.factretriever.com/spider-facts

13 Jimenez, Alberto Corsin. Spanish National Research Council, *Spider web anthropology's: ecologies, infrastructures, entanglement's,* http://digital.csic.es/bitstream/10261/134351/1/spiderweb%20anthros_160209.pdf

Yet, fragile and frail, it is quickly swept away to nothingness by a child's finger!

Fatal or fragile? Bewildered, I realized the answer all depended on the one going through it.

3.
THE VENOMOUS KISS

A spider's fangs are natural injection needles, making them perfectly suited for piercing the skeletons of prey and delivering a kiss of venom.[14]

In the same way, satan's toothy barbs are perfectly suited for piercing his prey's skeleton—our minds or thought life—and delivering a venomous kiss. A kiss is defined as a touch of the lips or mouth. The touch of his mouth delivers venom. His words and suggestions are deadly.

In Ephesians 6, we're told to put on the whole armour of God. But with a list of many armour items to put on, *there's only one weapon of the enemy listed.* His method of attack is a fiery dart.

14 DNEWS. *Spider Fangs Make Perfect Injection Needles.* https://www.seeker.com/spider-fangs-make-perfect-injection-needles-1768601045.html

Above all, taking the shield of faith, wherewith ye shall be able to quench all the ***fiery darts of the wicked.***
Ephesians 6:16

Why is there only one weapon listed? We find the reason in Hebrews 2:14. This verse states that Jesus shared our humanity (He became human, a partaker of flesh and blood) so that:

...through death he [Jesus] might ***destroy*** *...* ***the devil;***
Hebrews 2:14

Destroy is the Greek word [katargeo] which means: to render entirely useless, and to render entirely idle. Jesus [katargeo]'d the devil! This is an extremely powerful revelation. Jesus used death as a weapon, and the devil was *rendered entirely useless.* Rendered entirely idle, there's very little he can do and very little he can attack us with. **His only weapon is a fiery dart.** We gain insight about these fiery darts when we read a verse preceding Ephesians 6:16.

Put on the whole armour of God, that ye may be able to stand against the wiles of the devil.
Ephesians 6:11

We put on armour so we can withstand the "wiles" of the devil. *Wiles* appears two times in Scripture. In Ephesians 6, it's the Greek word [methodeia], which reminds us of, and is similar to, our English word *method.* We must be able to withstand the method the enemy uses against us. But *wiles* is first mentioned in Numbers 25:18, which gives great insight into the meaning of the word and the very basis of its intent.

> *For they vex you with their wiles...*
> *Numbers 25:18*

Here, *wiles* is the Hebrew word [nekel] which means: deceit. This verse also tells us that wiles were used to *vex* the people. Vex [tsarar] means: to cramp. Wiles or deceit cramped, hindered, and impeded the people. (Sounds like they were caught in a trap to me.) So the method the enemy uses to cramp, hinder, and impede us (or wrap us up in his web) is a *method of deceit.* He uses this tactic against all people everywhere.

> ...the devil has waged war against God and truth for thousands of years. He fights this war on many fronts, and his primary weapon is lies. The devil has been inculcating lies into the human psyche and society for so long that there are lies deeply embedded...[15]

15 *Truth or Tradition?* https://www.truthortradition.com/articles/why-does-the-truth-offend

> ...all the promises are to the believer, if you were the devil what would you mess with? The belief system of a believer.[16]
>
> —Todd White

> Lies are the only real power demons have...[17]
>
> —Blake Healy

The method that the enemy uses is a method of deceit.

Satan spins a web simply because it's an easy way to catch prey without having to expend a lot of energy.

> Webs allow a spider to catch prey without having to expend energy by running it down.[18]

> When the spider pierces its prey with the fang, it squeezes out the venom, injecting the animal with enough neurotoxin to paralyze or kill. This makes it

16 White, Todd. *Coming Back to Your First Love.* https://www.youtube.com/watch?v=FuFHDfbjo2M (24:09)

17 Healy, Blake. *The Veil.* Charisma House, Charisma Media/Charisma House Book Group, Lake Mary, FL. 2018. Pg 35.

18 Wikipedia, s.v. "*Spider web.*" https://en.wikipedia.org/wiki/Spider_web

> safe for the spider to feed on its prey, without the risk of a struggle.[19]

The enemy definitely doesn't want a struggle. **He has been rendered entirely useless!** He's already been defeated, and he knows about his defeat better than we do—because he was there. Having been rendered entirely useless, satan uses his mouth to capture us.

> *...the age-old serpent who is called the devil and Satan ... continually* ***deceives*** *and* ***seduces*** *the entire inhabited world...*
>
> *Revelation 12:9 (AMP)*

> [Snakes] often move by twisting. And so the nature of evil is to twist. A lie is the twisting of the truth. The impure is the twisting of the pure. And evil, itself, is the twisting of the good.[20]
>
> —Jonathan Cahn

Satan's lies and deceits are fiery darts!

<u>Fiery:</u> The word *fiery* indicates poisonous. It's indicative of the venom of snakes and scorpions (spiders).

19 Harris, Tom. *How Spiders Work.* https://animals.howstuffworks.com/arachnids/spider7.htm

20 Cahn, Jonathan. *The Book of Mysteries.* (Lake Mary, FL: FrontLine, 2016.), pg. 10. Used by permission

> *...that great and terrible wilderness, wherein were* ***fiery serpents, and scorpions****...*
>
> *Deuteronomy 8:15*

Dart: A dart is a small arrow that is double-edged and sharp on both sides like a sword. Darts, in scripture, denote words!

> *...* ***tongues*** *are sharp swords.*
>
> *Psalm 57:4 (NIV)*

> *They sharpen their tongues like swords and aim* ***cruel words*** *like deadly arrows.*
>
> *Psalm 64:3 (NIV)*

> *They make ready their tongue like a bow, to shoot* ***lies****...*
>
> *Jeremiah 9:3 (NIV)*

Ironically, in another non-coincidental similarity:

> [the] Spider is associated with words and communication.[21]

Words and communication come from satan's mouth delivering a kiss to our souls, a kiss that releases a poisonous toxicity.

21 Phillips, Trish. *More Animal Symbolism.* http://www.pure-spirit.com/more-animal-symbolism/664-spider-symbolism

> … Their [Spiders'] mouthparts … act to manipulate …[22]

Satan's tongue manipulates, influences, exploits, and controls! His tongue aims cruel words; his tongue shoots treacherous lies. His lethal communication is intended to inject a deadly venom. His scheme is that fiery darts of subversive words and lies pierce through our skeletal skull and attach to, or attack, our minds.

His lethal communication is intended to inject a deadly venom.

> Spider webs are not passive traps. Instead, because of electrically conducive glue spread across their surface, webs spring towards their prey.[23]

Bitter words are hurled at our souls from the mouth of the enemy. We are bombarded by venomous thoughts of fear, depression, quitting, greed, lust, jealousy, perversion, abortion, addiction, suicide, self-harm… The list is long, and the list is deadly.

> Remember: Every web begins with a single thread … the spider climbs to a suitable starting point …

22 Richman, Richard. *Do spiders have tongues?* http://www.madsci.org/posts/archives/2000-12/977577464.Gb.r.html

23 Lehnardt, Karin. *84 Amazing Facts about Spiders.* https://www.factretriever.com/spider-facts

> and releases a length of thread into the wind. With any luck, the free end of the thread will catch on to another branch. If the spider feels that the thread has caught onto something, it cinches up the silk and attaches the thread to the starting point.[24]

Satan strategically releases his demonic, invisible, fiery darts in the form of venomous thoughts quickly whispered into our souls. The web-spinning spider has a strategic plan to manipulate our thinking. If we let the fiery thoughts of the enemy remain in our hearts and minds, we become susceptible to his plans and ideas. This becomes the access point that allows the enemy in. As his web attaches onto our soul, he quickly cinches up the thread and starts to weave.

> By weaving, [the spider] gains a certain element of control; once the prey is wrapped up, this control is complete.[25]

His venomous thoughts are whispered in hope that his thoughts will become our thoughts, thereby causing our thoughts to influence our actions.

> This influence is a spiritual force that twists and taints and pollutes God's ways. It is like a spiderweb,

24 Harris, Tom. *How Spiders Work.* https://animals.howstuffworks.com/arachnids/spider5.htm

25 Phillips, Trish. *More Animal Symbolism.* http://www.pure-spirit.com/more-animal-symbolism/664-spider-symbolism

and people get stuck in it. Writhing in their captivity, they act out of a "web mentality."[26]

—James Goll

...if you don't pay attention to the little things that are damaging and the little things that are twisting stuff around, then it's only a matter of time until these little things become really big things.[27]

—Todd White

You, with your thoughts, create a[n] ... environment with signals that change your blood chemistry. So ... the thought you're thinking now is generating an electrical and quantum signal throughout your whole brain, your entire body. So that the whole signal of your environment of the cells of your body—all 75-100 trillion of them—is being changed by how you are thinking now.[28]

—Dr. Carolyn Leaf

26 Goll, James. *Elijah List: It's Time This Thing Gets Exposed.* Encounters Network, The Elijah List, Nov 29, 2017. http://www.elijahlist.com/words/display_word.html?ID=19246

27 White, Todd. *When Finances are Stolen.* https://www.youtube.com/watch?v=o4ZtHyJ8Cq8 (24:50)

28 Leaf, Dr. Carolyn. *How To Detox Your Brain Part 2.* https://www.youtube.com/watch?v=iqQoJRoZj5Q (11:07)

Lust is conceived in the mind. If you don't deal with the toxic thoughts the enemy shoots at you, then they become more than thoughts—they become actions bringing forth sin through the deeds of the body.

> Spider fangs make perfect injection needles. Toothy barbs are perfectly suited for piercing the skeletons of prey…[29]

So again, the enemy's toothy barbs (fiery darts) are perfectly suited for piercing his prey's skeleton (mind or thought life). His venom is radical.

> Delivered through stiletto-sharp fangs, spider venom shuts down a victim's central nervous system, rendering it paralyzed—or dead—so the spider can turn its innards to mush and gulp down the organ soup.[30]
>
> And since Satan cannot assault God directly, he attacks God's friends. He tries to undermine the ground beneath your feet. The devil tries to paralyze your planning, abort your dreams and dilute your

29 *Spider Fangs Make Perfect Injection Needles.* https://www.seeker.com/spider-fangs-make-perfect-injection-needles-1768601045.html

30 Stockton, Nick. *The Secret History of Spider Venom's Paralytic Power.* https://www.wired.com/2015/06/secret-origin-spectacular-spider-venom/

> hope. He opposes everything that could help you stay close to God's heart.[31]
>
> —James Goll

His vonom is radical.

King David broke the commandments of God, and it all started with a thought—a lustful thought. A fiery dart hurled from the weaver-of-the-web enticed the fearless, faithful warrior and king. Temptation had come. It was a single strand of web that caught onto his soul then was cinched up and became the starting point of a sin that would lead to death—many deaths.

> *...every man is tempted, when he is drawn away of his own lust, and enticed.*
>
> *James 1:14*

The Greek word for *lust* in this verse is [epithumia] meaning: longing or desire. The Greek word for *enticed* is [deleazo] meaning: to entrap. Entrap is exactly what a web does. As the web confines and entangles us, the enemy wraps us up and injects his venom. Venom affects the central nervous system, which consists of mainly two parts: the brain

31 Goll, James. *Elijah List: How to Overcome Satan's 4 Favorite Tactics.* Encounters Network, The Elijah List, Aug 31, 2016. http://www.elijahlist.com/words/display_word.html?ID=16560

and the spine. It's a complex network that carries messages from the brain to various parts of the body.

> Researchers generally think the toxins slot into the same structures on the outside of a neuron that those nerve cells use to *communicate* ... venom hacks the network, shutting down *intercellular communications.* Result: paralysis and death.[32]

As in King David's experience, the sting of sin shut down his nerve cells used to communicate. His brain was no longer sending the proper signals to the rest of his body. Cinched up tight, the web thread was pulling David away from the God he so loved. He went from God-focused to self-focused. The fiery arrow that King David allowed to linger in his soul ejected its venom, causing God's passionate worshipper to go from spiritually-minded to carnally-minded.

> *For to be carnally minded is death...*
>
> *Romans 8:6*

> The greatest battle for your soul is between your ears. ...What you don't do is allow that thought to reside there. ...Control how long you dwell on them, how long you allow them to reside in your mind. ...It's just a thought and it will die, but you can't feed it!

32 Stockton, Nick. *The Secret History of Spider Venom's Paralytic Power.* https://www.wired.com/2015/06/secret-origin-spectacular-spider-venom/

> ...The real battle that's taking place is the battle for our minds.[33]
>
> —Jentezen Franklin

Isaiah the prophet gave us some good advice:

> *Let the wicked forsake his way, and the unrighteous man his* ***thoughts****...*
>
> *Isaiah 55:7*

The unrighteous thought is a web strand that offers a *promissory* world of entanglement. But remember, it's only promissory. Satan is a liar and will *never* deliver on what he has promised. Although the web *looks* vibrant and beautiful, it's *always* tensed with violence and catastrophe. He makes sin look pleasurable. He makes evil seem enjoyable. He makes wickedness seductively appealing. His desire is to lure us into his trap with a "promise" of pleasure, but **all sin leads to death**.

> *There is a way that seemeth right unto a man, but the end thereof are the ways of death.*
>
> *Proverbs 14:12* **(and)*** *Proverbs 16:25*

33 Franklin, Jentezen. *Spirit of Python: Snake Eggs in Your Head.* https://www.youtube.com/watch?v=HW8JGWAd0N0 (2:20) (5:30) (6:00) (10:42) (25:00)

*(Again, we see God place an exclamation mark or two after a phrase He repeats twice.) King David's immoral thoughts definitely had the promise of pleasure, seemed enjoyable, and were seductively appealing.

Instead of forsaking his unrighteous thoughts, King David was consumed by them. The passionate worshipper of the Lord had his inter-"cellular" communication hacked, shutting down his inter-"spirit-to-spirit" communion with the Lover of his soul.

> Operating in the flesh (not in the Spirit) is the conduit that allows curses to flow into our lives.[34]
>
> —Ken and Jean Harrington

As the kiss of death is delivered and venom runs through our blood, all desire to communicate with our Saviour is shut down. We become unable, or unwilling, to call out for help because our communications network is hacked. We withdraw and isolate ourselves from the very Source of life. Disconnected from our source of life, we're rendered powerless and paralyzed, making us easy prey for the devourer.

James describes the sequence of events:

But every man is tempted, when he is:

1. *drawn away of his own lust,*

34 Harrington, Ken and Jeanne. *From Curses to Blessings*, Destiny Image Publishers, Inc. Shippensburg, PA. 2011. Pg 36.

2. *and enticed.*
3. *Then when lust hath conceived,*
4. *it bringeth forth sin:*
5. *and sin, when it is finished, bringeth forth death.*

James 1:14–15 (phrased in point form)

See this sequence of events play out in King David's life.

1. **Drawn by lust:** The fiery dart pierces King David when he sees Bathsheba and begins to have a longing or desire.
2. **Enticed:** Instead of taking his thoughts captive, he allows them to remain, leading to entrapment or entanglement. With every thought, another strand of web is weaved around his soul making escape more and more difficult.
3. **Lust conceives:** King David conceives a plan of action that will enable him to act on his enticingly pleasurable thoughts.
4. **Sin:** Fiery thoughts lead to sinful action. King David commits the sin.
5. **Death:** His sin leads to death, many deaths—the death of Uriah (Bathsheba's husband); the death of their child; and, ultimately, the death of Absalom and Adonijah years later. Due to the guilt and shame of what he had done, King David—very adept at ruling a nation—could not properly rule his own household

in the area of disciplining his children. *(And his father had not displeased him at any time in saying, Why hast thou done so? [1 Kings 1:6])* Therefore, even years later, rebellion rooted in David's sin with Bathsheba sprouted up in the household of the king, resulting in the death of Absalom and Adonijah. The wages of sin is death!

...the motions of sins ... bring forth fruit unto death.
Romans 7:5

> I'm telling you, if you give satan an inch he will take not a mile, he will take your life! If you give him just a little bit, he'll take your everything! This is not a joke. This is not a place to play games. It's not compromise—so this little stuff: this pornography, this little bit of addiction, this little bit of this, this little bit of that— it's not okay! It is ruining you inside and what happens is it starts to sear your conscience and then all of a sudden you shipwrecked your faith.[35]
>
> —Todd White

It's very important for us to understand that God never tempts us!

35 White, Todd. *When Finances are Stolen.* https://www.youtube.com/watch?v=o4ZtHyJ8Cq8 (38:40)

> *Let no one say when he is tempted, I am being tempted by God; for God cannot be tempted by evil, and He Himself does not tempt anyone.*
>
> *James 1:13 (NASB)*

> **What we have to do is recognize that sin is voluntary.** No one forces you and me to sin. Sin is a choice that we make (Ecclesiastes 7:29). He made us perfect but we choose. We choose with our mind whether we are going to listen to God's advice on whatever we are thinking about to do or we are ignoring God, listening to our own advice or listening to the lies of the enemy.[36]
>
> —Dr. Carolyn Leaf

Every lie of the enemy is a dart that offers a beguiling temptation. With every temptation comes a choice. Sin is voluntary, meaning it's optional, non-compulsive, and discretionary. It's up to the individual. We can choose to forsake the devious thoughts of iniquity—in other words, "quench the fiery dart"—or we can commit the sin.

> *But remember this—the wrong desires that come into your life aren't anything new and different. Many others have faced exactly the same problems before you. And* ***no***

36 Leaf, Dr. Carolyn. *How To Detox Your Brain Part 2*. https://www.youtube.com/watch?v=iqQoJRoZj5Q (6:47)

> ***temptation is irresistible**. You can trust God to keep the temptation from becoming so strong that you can't stand up against it, for he has promised this and will do what he says.* ***He will show you how to escape*** *temptation's power so that you can bear up patiently against it.*
>
> *1 Corinthians 10:13 (TLB)*

Know this: the dart itself is not the sin but is meant to cause us to sin. With every temptation there *is* a way of escape—that is a promise from God!

> It is not a sin to be tempted. We can't help … when we have thoughts randomly that just come at us. … but what you don't do is allow that thought to reside there and stay there…[37]
>
> —Jentezen Franklin

> Questions are allowed in the kingdom, but lack of answers must not interrupt our heart–communion with God.[38]
>
> —Bill Johnson

37 Franklin, Jentezen. *Spirit of Python: Snake Eggs in Your Head.* https://www.youtube.com/watch?v=HW8JGWAd0N0 (5:15)

38 Johnson, Bill. *The War in Your Head.* Destiny Image Publishers, Inc. Shippensburg, PA. 2014. Pg 38.

When we entertain the thought, the enemy capitalizes on it. It's vital that we prosper in our souls. This is why God said that we must:

> *...take every thought captive to make it obey Christ.*
> *2 Corinthians 10:5 (NET)*

Satan's web (the fiery dart, the wrong desire, the temptation) is not passive. It springs at you, his prey. Learn to recognize the fiery darts and extinguish them before they poison you. Satan's diabolical web was designed to manipulate, control, and ultimately kill you! His intent is to kiss you with fiery venom. If he can entice you to sin, his plan has succeeded, because sin is the sting of death.

> *The sting of death is sin...*
> *1 Corinthians 15:56*

4. JESUS—AS SERPENT?

There are many prophetic pictures of our Messiah in the Old Testament. Jesus Christ is the reality, or very image, of the Old Testament shadows represented by many places, animals, and things (e.g. Shiloh, lamb, Passover, ram, bull, red heifer, dove, veil).

> *...things which are a mere shadow of what is to come; but* ***the substance belongs to Christ****.*
>
> *Colossians 2:16–17 (NASB)*

Shiloh: The sceptre shall not depart from Judah ... until Shiloh [Shiyloh] come... (Genesis 49:10). [Shiyloh]: an epithet of the Messiah.[39]

39 Staggs, Brandon. SwordSearcher, *Interlinear KJV with Strong's Greek & Hebrew Lexicon.* iPhone app. Apple App Store. Vers. 3.4. Brandon Staggs, 1999.

Lamb: ...Behold the Lamb of God, which taketh away the sin of the world (John 1:29).

Passover: ...For even Christ our passover is sacrificed for us: (1 Corinthians 5:7).

Ram: ...a ram for peace offerings... (Leviticus 9:4).

Goat: ...bring the goat ... and offer him for a sin offering (Leviticus 16:9).

Bull: ...carry forth the bullock without the camp ... it is a sin offering for the congregation (Leviticus 4:21).

Red Heifer: ...bring thee a red heifer without spot, wherein is no blemish ... bring her forth without the camp, and one shall slay her ... it is a purification for sin (Numbers 19:2–3,9).

Turtledove: ...he shall bring for his trespass, which he hath committed, two turtledoves... (Leviticus 5:7).

Veil: Having ... boldness to enter into the holiest ... through the veil, that is to say, his flesh... (Hebrews 10:19–20).

Jesus Christ: He is our Messiah, the Lamb of God, our Passover, our peace offering, our sin offering, our purification from sin, our trespass offering, the veil we enter through to God. The Old Testament was a shadow. Christ is the perfect, real image!

Yet when Jesus referred to Himself while speaking to Nicodemus, He didn't refer to any of these innocent shadows. Jesus didn't allude to Himself as lamb or dove, but He connected Himself to a ***snake***! Jesus linked Himself, the Son of Man, to the brazen serpent that Moses lifted up in the wilderness to bring healing to a people deep in rebellion and sin. Jesus maintained that He was in the place of the snake—the portrayal of evil and the curse.

The serpent had tricked Eve into sinning, causing her to disobey God and eat from the Tree of Knowledge of Good **and Evil**. Adam and Eve already had knowledge of good. They were in a state of perfection: taking care of the garden, naming the animals, communing with God who is the Spirit of Knowledge (Isaiah 11:2). What they were about to gain from this tree was the knowledge of evil. *Evil* is the Hebrew word [ra]—a short word with huge implications. The list of meanings from this tiniest of words is huge. Here's a list that is by no means exhaustive:

Ra:[40]

evil (natural or moral)	distress	ill	trouble
bad	evil	ill-favoured	vex
adversity	grief	mischief	wickedness
affliction	harm	misery	wrong
calamity	hurt	sad	worse(-st)
displeasure	hurtful	sorrow	

40 Staggs, Brandon. SwordSearcher, *Interlinear KJV with Strong's Greek & Hebrew Lexicon.* iPhone app. Apple App Store. Vers. 3.4. Brandon Staggs, 1999.

This is what they would gain—and it would be the worse(st)! Adam and Eve had only known good—beautiful, best, bountiful, cheerfulness, graciousness, kindness, pleasure, prosperity, well-favour.[41] But sin carries a sting; it brings a curse, a fallen state—a lower position.

Adam and Eve already had knowledge of good. What they were about to gain from this tree was the knowledge of evil.

Jesus wanted Nicodemus—and therefore the world—to know there was a cure. The cure that He would procure could be dramatically seen in the Old Testament shadow—the story of Moses lifting up a brazen serpent on a pole in the wilderness.

Let's look at the story found in Numbers 21.

> *And the people spake against God, and against Moses, Wherefore have ye brought us up out of Egypt to die in the wilderness? for there is no bread, neither is there any water; and our soul loatheth this light bread.*
>
> *And the Lord sent fiery serpents among the people, and they bit the people; and much people of Israel died.*

41 Staggs, Brandon. SwordSearcher, *Interlinear KJV with Strong's Greek & Hebrew Lexicon.* iPhone app. Apple App Store. Vers. 3.4. Brandon Staggs, 1999.

> *Therefore the people came to Moses, and said, We have sinned, for we have spoken against the Lord, and against thee; pray unto the Lord, that he take away the serpents from us. And Moses prayed for the people.*
>
> *And the Lord said unto Moses, Make thee a fiery serpent, and set it upon a pole: and it shall come to pass, that every one that is bitten, when he looketh upon it, shall live.*
>
> *And Moses made a serpent of brass, and put it upon a pole, and it came to pass, that if a serpent had bitten any man, when he beheld the serpent of brass, he lived.*
>
> *Numbers 21:5–9*

In this Scripture, we see that God gave Moses the antidote for the venomous bite of the serpent. (Notice that sin was the reason for the bite.) Moses was to take some brass and shape it into the form of what was killing them; then when they looked *up* at it, it would save them. The people would need to have a **steadfast ability** to *look up* at what was *lifted up.*

Could they look up at the brazen serpent while snakes slithered all around them … bit them … crawled on them … writhed over them? Could they continue to look at the lifeless serpent lifted up on a pole rather than on the twisting, vicious serpents slithering up their legs and twisting around their beloved children? Could they continue to look up while their feet, arms, and faces were swelling and burning in excruciating pain from the venom coursing through their bodies? Could they continue to look up while family and friends screamed desperately for help? Could they continue to look up while trying to convince their babies to keep their eyes focused on the snake that was lifted up, and not on the snake hissing below?

The serpent bit, don't look …

Their legs were swelling, don't look …

Their pain was intense, don't look …

Their minds were frantic, don't look …

Their babies were crying, don't look …

Their young were hysterical, don't look …

Their families were dying, don't look …

> The people would need to have a steadfast ability to *look up* at what was *lifted up*.

Excruciating pain, grotesque swelling, venom-induced hemorrhaging—the verdict was fatal. **In their crisis and distress, they needed to look up at the brass serpent on the pole in order to be healed—in order to live!**

And as Moses lifted up the serpent in the wilderness, even so must the Son of man be lifted up:

John 3:14

Jesus revealed to Nicodemus that He (Jesus) would be like that serpent of brass. This, too, was symbolic. *Brass* in Hebrew is [nechosheth] and it means: brass, copper, or steel. It also means: **lust, harlotry**; and is also translated as: **filthiness, chains, fetters…**[42]

In an exact carbon copy of the Old Testament shadow, Jesus Christ, our Messiah, became what was killing us. What was killing us? ➔ Sin (evil). [Ra] was killing us! Man had partaken of the Tree of Knowledge of Good and [Ra], and a curse descended on the earth. Jesus had to become the curse to purchase our salvation.

He became the curse: *…being made a curse for us… (Galatians 3:13).*

He became sin: *…he made him to be sin who knew no sin… (2 Corinthians 5:21, ESV).*

He became all the evil ever to be known! He became like whatever bit you: cancer, depression, AIDS, abuse, crime, hatred, envy, starvation, STDs… He became every vile, putrid evil there was, is, or ever will be. *He became sin to produce the cure!*

Jesus Christ was formed into the shape of what was killing us! —And whoever looks upon Him shall live and have everlasting life. When we look *up* at the cross, we see the holy, unblemished Lamb of God. But when Jesus looks *down* at

42 Sowing Circle. Blue Letter Bible, *Interlinear Concordance.* iPhone app. Apple App Store. Vers. 2.54. Sowing Circle. 2016.

the cross, He sees all the sins of humanity. He declared, "I'm like that serpent on the pole, and those who look upon me shall live." This was the real reason He came to earth—to become the curse so that we could be redeemed. The Son of Man would be—no, *must* be—lifted up in the form of what was killing us to become our salvation. We had been stung with a venomous sting, but **Jesus Christ delivered the antivenom**.

5.
ANTIVENOM DELIVERED

Due to the law-of-first-mention, the serpent was a symbol of the curse. As discussed previously, *curse* is first mentioned in Genesis 3:14, where the serpent was cursed for allowing satan to use his body in order to carry out his deception on humankind.

> *And the Lord God said unto the serpent, Because thou hast done this, thou art cursed…*
>
> *Genesis 3:14*

Immediately, the first Messianic prophecy came. God promised the serpent (satan) that the woman he just deceived would have seed, and her seed would crush his head! Jesus Christ is the woman's seed and the destroyer of her foe.

And I will put enmity between you and the woman, and between your offspring and hers; he will crush your head...

Genesis 3:15 (NIV)

Note the address of the Old Testament scripture regarding the first mention of *curse*—Genesis **3:14**. In keeping with the precision and accuracy of God's character, He mentions the antivenom for the curse in the New Testament verse—John **3:14**.

Genesis 3:14		John 3:14
Curse	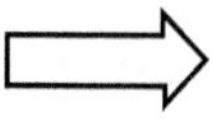	Antivenom
"Thou art cursed..."		*"As Moses lifted up the serpent..."*

And as Moses lifted up the serpent in the wilderness, even so must the Son of man be lifted up:

John 3:14

The cure for the curse would be found in Jesus being lifted up "as" Moses lifted up the serpent in the wilderness. *As* means: in the same way. Antivenom would be formulated *as* Jesus was lifted up.

And I, if I be lifted up from the earth, will draw all men unto me.

John 12:32

Let's take a look at antivenom in the natural realm so we can see how it works in the spiritual realm.

> *For the invisible things … are … understood by the things that are made…*
>
> *Romans 1:20*

The making of antivenom from snakes and spiders is very similar. We will look at both, focusing on the snake since Jesus referred to being lifted up as the brazen serpent.

How is antivenom made? **Antivenom is made from venom!**

> Antivenom is made by collecting venom from the relevant animal… Versions are available for *spider* bites, *snake* bites … and *scorpion* stings.[43]
>
> **Any good antivenom starts with its opposite.**[44]

To make life-saving antivenom…

> Step 1: A technician extracts and later **purifies** the venom from the species for which scientists want to make an antivenom.[45]

43 Wikipedia. "*Antivenom.*" https://en.wikipedia.org/wiki/Antivenom

44 Wade, Lizzie. *Here's How You Milk Snakes To Make Antivenom.* https://www.wired.com/2014/11/how-to-make-antivenum/

45 *Biting Back.* https://www.aaas.org/sites/default/files/sw-091613-biting-back.pdf

> Herpetologists do the milking, **forcing** the snake to bite down … so that venom drips from its fangs.[46]

In like manner, spiders are also milked.

> Spiders are milked to collect their venom, which is used to create antivenom to treat poisonous spider bites.[47]

This is called "milking venom." A snake must be "milked" in order to collect the venom. The snake is milked of its poison. This is the only effective way to obtain the venom, and it's vital in order to produce an antivenom.

> [He] grips the snake's head between his bare fingers and carefully guides it toward a cup… the snake strikes at the cup, piercing the film with its fangs and spraying its venom into the container below.[48]

It's interesting to note that humans have NO natural immunity to venom!

> There are some animals who have more resilience to certain venomous species, **humans don't**. …there is no natural immunity to [venom] in humans. …**an**

46 Wade, Lizzie. *Here's How You Milk Snakes To Make Antivenom.* https://www.wired.com/2014/11/how-to-make-antivenum/

47 *Milking Spiders For Their Venom.* https://www.terminix.com/blog/science-nature/milking-spiders-for-their-venom/

48 *Biting Back.* https://www.aaas.org/sites/default/files/sw-091613-biting-back.pdf

> **external source** of antibodies **is needed** to counter the effect of venom.[49]

Did you catch that? Humans have no natural immunity, but … certain animals do!

> …Sheep and goats are such mammals who are resilient to venoms.[50]

Jesus Christ, the *Lamb* of God, takes away my sin (the bite of the viper). Jesus Christ was provided as the offering for my sin (the sting of death).

> Any good antivenom starts with its opposite!

The next step in making antivenom is to inject it into a domestic animal's blood.

> The process involves injecting live venomous fluid in any of these animals. Their immunity helps produce antibodies who can diffuse a live venomous cell.[51]

> A small amount of spider venom is injected into animals such as … **sheep** … The animals' immune

49 *How Does Antivenom Work in Our Bodies When Injected.* Quora. https://www.quora.com/How-does-anti-venom-work-in-our-bodies-when-injected

50 *How Does Antivenom Work in Our Bodies When Injected.* Quora. https://www.quora.com/How-does-anti-venom-work-in-our-bodies-when-injected

51 *How Does Antivenom Work in Our Bodies When Injected.* Quora. https://www.quora.com/How-does-anti-venom-work-in-our-bodies-when-injected

> system kicks in to protect them, creating antibodies. These antibodies are taken from the animals' blood and used to **make antivenom serum** for people.[52]

The venom-infused blood produces antibodies. An antibody is a *blood* protein produced in response to and counteracting a specific antigen or toxic/foreign substance. Then the blood containing the antibodies is drawn from the animal. The purified antivenom is now ready to be administered to venom-bitten people.

> Jesus became the curse in order to produce the cure

Remember: **Any good antivenom starts with its opposite!** Therefore, the antivenom *for* the curse had to be made *from* the curse. Jesus had to be lifted up from the earth as the brazen serpent—as every lust, harlotry, filth, chain, fetter, and curse—in order to produce our salvation. Jesus became the curse in order to produce the cure.

> *…Cursed is every one that hangeth on a tree:*
>
> *Galatians 3:13*

Jesus Christ "milked the snake," so to speak. He milked the serpent, satan, of his poison. It's important to notice that

52 *Milking Spiders For Their Venom.* https://www.terminix.com/blog/science-nature/milking-spiders-for-their-venom/

satan did NOT bite Jesus. Jesus had not committed any sin and therefore was never "bitten." Satan was *forcefully* milked by Jesus Christ. The lethal power from the fiery viper had been milked into a deadly cup. It's no wonder Jesus cried out with desperation:

> *...My Father, if it is possible, let this cup pass from me; yet not as I will, but as You will.*
>
> *Matthew 26:39 (NASB)*

> No longer do you have to drink the cup of trembling. It's paid for in full by your Redeemer.[53]
>
> —Mike Bickle

> *Thus saith thy Lord ... and thy God that pleadeth the cause of his people, Behold, I have taken out of thine hand the cup of trembling ...* ***thou shalt no more drink it again****:*
>
> *Isaiah 51:22*

Voluntarily, Jesus injected every bit of satan's potent venom into Himself—every sting of serpent and scorpion. Jesus drank the cup of raw venom forcefully milked from the lethal serpent, down to the very last drop. The deadly, potent venom was injected into our perfect, vital Passover Lamb. His immortal immune system kicked in to protect Him

53 Bickle, Mike. *Cultivating a Fiery Spirit.* CD Series

and generate antibodies. *His blood* produced antibodies in response to the toxic substance of the serpent's venom. The molecular structure of the live venomous cells was diffused.

His immortal immune system kicked in to protect Him and generate antibodies.

Purifying the deadly toxic cocktail, Jesus Christ created the perfect, vital antivenom for mankind in His blood!

6.

THE BRAZEN SERPENT BITES BACK

> **Step 6: When a patient comes in with a bite** or sting, doctors … inject antivenom… The antibodies circulate through the body and **neutralize** the toxin…[54]

The doctor administers the antivenom, but just how does antivenom work in our bodies when injected?

> Antivenom **binds** to the venom and chemically changes it to something that cannot interact with the body, thus **neutralizing** its effects.[55]

Jesus bound Himself to the venom, chemically changing it so that it cannot interact with your body. The venom had

54 *Biting Back.* https://www.aaas.org/sites/default/files/sw-091613-biting-back.pdf

55 *How Does Antivenom Work in Our Bodies When Injected.* Quora. https://www.quora.com/How-does-anti-venom-work-in-our-bodies-when-injected

been neutralized. Neutralize means to make something ineffective by applying an opposite force. In other words:

RENDERED ENTIRELY USELESS.

Why do we fear what's been defeated? Why do we cower from what's been overcome?

> Hundreds of thousands of people count snakes and spiders among their fears, …people tend to be exposed to a lot of negative information regarding snakes and spiders … this makes them more likely to be associated with phobia.[56]

Many have been filled with wrong information regarding satan and his power, giving them a fear or phobia of him and his doings. Fear comes from the devil. God has not given us the spirit of fear but of power (2 Timothy 1:7). Jesus came to destroy the works of the enemy through death itself. As a reminder, let's look again at Hebrews 2:14, where we read that Jesus [katargeo]'d the devil! The Son of Man was lifted up on a pole as the brazen serpent. Filled with all the infinite, indestructible power of heaven, the brazen serpent bit back. In true snake form, His bite-of-death paralyzed the demonic force, and the devil was *rendered entirely useless.*

56 *Science News, Unlocking The Psychology Of Snake And Spider Phobias,* https://www.sciencedaily.com/releases/2008/03/080320132646.htm

> *Forasmuch then as the children are partakers of flesh and blood, he also himself likewise took part of the same; that through death he might destroy … the devil;*
>
> *Hebrews 2:14*

Important note: satan's venom was not powerful enough to kill Christ! Venom does not kill the animal that produces the antivenom. Jesus willing laid His life down to destroy the devil and his works. He powerfully declared:

> *No one takes my life from me. I give it up willingly! I have the power to give it up and the power to receive it back again, just as my Father commanded me to do.*
>
> *John 10:18 (CEV)*

Again: satan's venom did not kill Christ! And, it's important to note that snakes don't just willingly spew their venom into a cup; rather, *grabbed* by the head, the snake is forcefully "guided" to a cup where the snake's glands are "pressed" to release their venom.

> **When the time is ripe**, professionals introduce the snakes … into a milking room. The snake is grabbed with the thumb and index finger at the very back of the head just behind the angle of the jaw where the venom glands reside. This allows the snake milker to

> press the snake's glands without allowing the snake to turn and bite.[57]

Notice that the snake is NOT ALLOWED to bite the milker! Jesus willingly drank the cup in order to produce an antivenom! Another important note: the snake has to be milked at the ripe time—meaning the right time! No wonder the Bible victoriously declares:

> *But when the **fulness of the time was come**, God sent forth his Son, made of a woman, made under the law, to redeem them that were under the law, that we might receive the adoption of sons.*
>
> *Galatians 4:4–5*

Not only did Jesus have to be born at the proper time and the snake-milking done at the proper time, but antivenom also needs to be administered on a timely basis.

> Proper first aid is of paramount importance in the life of a snake bite victim, especially in the first hour, also known as the "golden hour." Administering the correct antivenom on a timely basis will result in a 100% chance of survival.[58]

57 Puiu, Tibi. *Antivenom: how it's made and why it's so precious.* https://www.zmescience.com/other/feature-post/antivenom-made-precious/

58 Pereira, Dr. Anand & Geeta. *Antivenom: Why it's So Precious!* http://www.daijiworld.com/chan/exclusiveDisplay.aspx?articlesID=2609

Antivenom renders venom harmless! In the natural, antivenom can stop further damage but usually cannot undo damage already done. BUT … Jesus' blood is ***not*** the blood of mere animals. Jesus reversed the curse! God's perfect Lamb has blood *so* uncontaminated, *so* spotless, *so* purified… that even the works *already done* by the devil are destroyed!

> *…For this purpose the Son of God was manifested, that he might destroy the works of the devil.*
>
> *1 John 3:8*

Destroy in 1 John is a different Greek word than the one found in Hebrews 2. This destroy is [luo]: destroy, dissolve, melt.[59]

In other words, the One who received the bite, extracted the venom, and purified it is not only capable of fighting and destroying the venomous cells that you've been bitten with, but His blood—His antivenom—also [luo]'s those lethal cells: destroying and dissolving them completely; completely undoing any damage done by the venom.

> Notice a few things: (1) The serpent on the pole is … for bitten people (verse 8). The poison is in them, and without divine intervention they will die. (2) … The wrath of God is on this people for their sin… (3)

59 Staggs, Brandon. SwordSearcher, *Interlinear KJV with Strong's Greek & Hebrew Lexicon.* iPhone app. Apple App Store. Vers. 3.4. Brandon Staggs, 1999.

> The means God chooses to rescue the people from … [the] curse is a picture of the curse itself. (4) All they have to do in order to be saved … is look at his provision hanging on a pole.[60]

Turn your eyes upon Jesus! Turn away from the natural realm and fasten your gaze on the One who has conquered all!

> *For this is the will of My Father, that everyone who **beholds the Son** and believes in Him will have eternal life…*
>
> *John 6:40 (NASB)*

60 Piper, John. *Desiring God.* https://www.desiringgod.org/messages/the-son-of-man-must-be-lifted-up-like-the-serpent

7.
LORD OF THE CURSE

Humankind was stung with a sting! Without divine intervention, we would die.

> Sickness and death are a result of the fall of man and the consequent curse that was imposed upon creation. Yet "Christ has redeemed us from the curse of the law, being made a curse for us" (Galatians 3:13).[61]
>
> —Ken and Jean Harrington

As Jesus Christ, our Messiah, was lifted up on the cross, He wore a crown of thorns. Thorns are a symbol of the curse. Once again, we see two vastly different words representing the same thing—crown, thorns.

---

61 Harrington, Ken and Jeanne. From Curses to Blessings, Destiny Image Publishers, Inc. Shippensburg, PA. 2011. Pg 35.

> Think about it, a crown, a symbol of royalty, power, kingship, wealth and glory … yet made not of gold or jewels, but of thorns. Why? When man fell the consequence of that fall was the curse; the ground would now bare thorns and thistles. The thorns were thus the sign of the curse, the sign of a fallen world…[62]
>
> —Jonathan Cahn

The one who knew no sin came to *be* sin. Pierced to redeem us, He set us free from the web of the enemy. He allowed Himself to be pierced with the venom of the devourer so that we could receive life, health, joy, and peace—everything exactly opposite to what we receive while caught in the enemy's web. Jesus Christ is King of the pierced—He became King of those pierced by the devourer's venomous fangs.

> When a crown is placed on a man's head, he becomes king. At that moment, the weight of the kingdom rests upon him…
>
> He [the Messiah] became… the King of Thorns. Thorns speak of pain and tears. So the crown of thorns means he will now bear the pain and tears of men. Thorns speak of piercing. So he will be pierced. And the thorns are linked to the curse and the curse is linked to death. …the crown of thorns ordains that

62 Cahn, Jonathan. The Book of Mysteries. (Lake Mary, FL: FrontLine, 2016.), pg. 25. Used by permission

> Messiah will die. He will bear the weight of the curse upon his head. He becomes the king of thorns, the king of the curse.
>
> ...the crown also signifies authority ... One who reigns.
>
> ...thus by bearing the weight of the curse, He becomes king over it. He becomes King of the Curse. And King of the Cursed.
>
> King of the Broken, King of the Pierced and Wounded, King of the Rejected and King of Tears. So all who have fallen can come to Him and find redemption.[63]
>
> —Jonathan Cahn

The fallen ones—we all have fallen. Romans 3:23 states that all have sinned. Every person has sinned and has come under the curse. In the book of Daniel, we see another 9-1-1 verse.

> *...therefore the curse has been poured out on us ... because we have sinned against him.*
>
> *Daniel 9:11 (AMPC)*

63 Cahn, Jonathan. *The Book of Mysteries.* (Lake Mary, FL: FrontLine, 2016.), pg. 25. Used by permission

The sting of death is sin! You can do nothing to protect yourself against the enemy's venom. All you can do is look to the cross. That is where the life-saving antivenom is found. Interestingly, when antivenom is given:

> This is a form of Passive immunity.[64]

Passive means: *accept* what happens or what others do without active response. It also denotes the subject undergoing the action of the verb. YOU, the subject, must undergo the action or the accomplishment of what Jesus did for you on the cross. **He** executed all the action! **He** took your sin, **He** produces the antibodies to fight death's sting, **He** purifies the venom (the sin). We, as humans, have no natural immunity to satan's venom. There's nothing we can do except to *accept* what Christ has done for us.

> The hardest thing to get a person with a religious spirit to do is simply *accept* the new beginning and push delete.[65]
>
> —Mike Bickle

Replete with life, His blood is so full of antibodies that it counteracts and neutralizes the sting of death. His blood totally sets us free from the sting of death—*if* we behold the Son of God upon the cross.

64 *How Does Antivenom Work in Our Bodies When Injected.* Quora. https://www.quora.com/How-does-anti-venom-work-in-our-bodies-when-injected

65 Bickle, Mike. *Cultivating a Fiery Spirit.* CD Series

...everyone who ***beholds the Son*** *and believes in Him will have eternal life...*

John 6:40 (NASB)

Looking unto Jesus *the author and finisher of our faith; who for the joy that was set before him endured the cross...*

Hebrews 12:2

That if thou shalt ***confess with thy mouth*** *the Lord Jesus, and shalt* ***believe in thine heart*** *that God hath raised him from the dead, thou shalt be saved.*

Romans 10:9

➔ADMINISTER ANTIVENOM: My friend, have you looked upon the One who took death's sting for you? *Everyone* has sinned and been bitten by the sting of death. We were born into sin because Adam and Eve were deceived by the serpent's "fiery darts"—his lying, beguiling words! Satan didn't wrestle them down with brute force, but with crafty manipulation of deceptive, alluring words he deceived them into the action of sin.

...Eve was deceived by the serpent's clever lies...

2 Corinthians 11:3 (TPT)

Eve listened to the illusory, deviously shrewd words that offered a "promise" of an even better life than the complete, absolute perfection they were living in. (That must have been quite the convincing conversation.) Consequently, Adam and Eve **chose** sin rather than obedience to their Father.

> *Wherefore, as by one man sin entered into the world, and death by sin; and so death passed upon all men, for that all have sinned:*
>
> *Romans 5:12*

We've all been caught in that cursed web of the enemy, but Jesus became a curse to set us free from satan's fatal trap. Without Christ, we are cinched into sin by the devil's web.

> *That's what happens to all who forget God—all their hopes come to nothing. They hang their life from one thin thread, they hitch their fate to a spider web.*
>
> *Job 8:13–14 (MSG)*

Never let the web determine your destiny!

Without choosing Christ, you allow the web to predetermine development of your life events. Never let the web determine your destiny! The determined factor is consistently the same—death! But when we *accept* and choose Jesus Christ as our Lord, His blood cleanses us and sets us free.

> *...the blood of Jesus Christ his Son cleanseth us from all sin.*
>
> *1 John 1:7*

His blood sets us free from the enemy's tangled web—the law of sin and death.

> *For the law of the Spirit of life in Christ Jesus hath made me free from the law of sin and death.*
>
> *Romans 8:2*

If you have never believed nor confessed Him as your Lord, today is a good day to be set free from the clutches and deadly bite of sin.

> *The fear of the Lord is a fountain of life, that one may turn away from the snares of death.*
>
> *Proverbs 14:27 (ESV)*

Jesus bore the weight of the curse! Jesus is the King of the curse. That means He owns the curse. Don't let the curse own you! He paid for your sin; therefore, He owns your sin. Don't let sin own you! Look to Jesus! He is the author of your faith! God has given to *every* man a measure of faith (Romans 12:3). That means that every single person has been enabled to receive salvation. We are saved by faith in Jesus Christ. *Whosoever* believes in Him will not perish! (John 3:16). Whosoever means: *any person*!

> *...whosoever shall call on the name of the Lord shall be saved.*
>
> *Acts 2:21* ***(and)*** ** Romans 10:13*

*(Again, God says the exact same thing twice—placing an exclamation point or two on this particular phrase.) God greatly loves you and has a great desire to see you delivered from death's sting.

> ***For this is the will of My Father**, that **everyone** who **beholds** the Son and **believes** in Him will have eternal life...*
>
> *John 6:40 (NASB)*

> ***The Lord is ... not willing** that any should perish, but that **all** should come to repentance.*
>
> *2 Peter 3:9*

He owns the curse.
Don't let the curse own you!

Father God's greatest desire is that everyone would behold His Son and live! His greatest desire is that we would receive the antivenom He delivered to the world at immeasurable cost—the cost of His Holy Son, His spotless Lamb! He promises you life everlasting. And, He always delivers on

His promises! Satan also desires to have you. Mercifully, we now know that his offer is a promissory world silhouetting beauty but tensed with violence and catastrophe. If you've never believed and received Jesus Christ, you're caught in the enemy's weaved web. Administer the proper first aid to your sting!

> Never forget: Proper first aid is of paramount importance in the life of a snake bite victim, especially in the first hour, also known as the "golden hour." Administering the correct antivenom on a timely basis will result in a 100% chance of survival.[66]

The result is a 100% chance of survival!

Today is your "golden hour!" If there is life, there is time! Administer the antivenom Jesus produced on your behalf. The result is a 100% chance of survival!

> *...the truth shall make you free.*
>
> *John 8:32*

Jesus declared that HE is the TRUTH! Therefore, He is the One who sets you free!

66 Pereira, Dr. Anand & Geeta. *Antivenom: Why it's So Precious!* http://www.daijiworld.com/chan/exclusiveDisplay.aspx?articlesID=2609

Jesus saith unto him, I am the way, the truth, and the life…

John 14:6

Believe in Jesus Christ and declare with your mouth, **"Jesus became the curse for me, purchasing my redemption and delivering me from sin. Jesus Christ is my Lord and Saviour!"**

Hallelujah! You have now been "made free from sin" (Romans 6:22) and delivered from sin's penalty, which is death. The Passion Translation says it so beautifully:

This "realm of death" describes our former state, for we were held in sin's grasp. But now, we've been resurrected out of that "realm of death" never to return, for we are forever alive and forgiven of all our sins!

He canceled out every legal violation we had on our record and the old arrest warrant that stood to indict us. He erased it all—our sins, our stained soul—he deleted it all ***and they cannot be retrieved****. Everything we once were in Adam has been placed onto his cross and nailed permanently there as a public display of cancellation.*

Then Jesus made a public spectacle of all the powers and principalities of darkness, stripping away from them every weapon and all their spiritual authority and power to accuse us. And by the power of the cross, Jesus

> *led them around as prisoners in a procession of triumph.*
> ***He was not their prisoner; they were his!***
> *Colossians 2:13–15 (TPT)*

Jesus was never satan's prisoner. The serpent-and-scorpion army of hell didn't take His life. They were nowhere near strong enough! Just one drop of His blood is more powerful than all the hordes of hell put together. He gladly laid His life down.

> *...Because his heart was focused on the joy of knowing that you would be his, he endured the agony...*
> *Hebrew 12:2 (TPT)*

He endured, knowing that He was producing the greatest antidote there ever would be, in order to procure His sons and daughters.

> *Now we're no longer living like slaves ... but we enjoy being God's very own sons and daughters!*
> *Galatians 4:7 (TPT)*

Welcome to being a child of God!

8.
ESCAPE ENTANGLEMENT

Salvation cost us nothing, yet cost heaven every-thing. Christ set us free at a great cost, lavishing on us His priceless, precious antivenom.

> *In him we have redemption through His blood, the forgiveness of sins … that he lavished on us…*
> *Ephesians 1:7–8 (NIV)*

As His children, we now have a responsibility to remain untangled and to stay out of satan's web.

> *For freedom did Christ **set us free**: stand fast therefore, and be not **entangled again** in a yoke of bondage.*
> *Galatians 5:1 (ASV)*

> *For if, **after they have escaped** the defilements of the world by the knowledge of the Lord and Savior Jesus*

> *Christ, they are **again entangled** in them and are overcome, the last state has become worse for them than the first.*
>
> *2 Peter 2:20 (NASB)*

As children of God, we've been set free from the sinful condition that we were born into and the sins that we've repented from. But as we continue on a day-to-day basis, the enemy continually releases single strands of web, hoping it will catch onto our souls, enabling him to wrap another small, almost invisible strand again and again until we're wrapped and trapped into sin once more.

Maybe you just received Christ as your personal Saviour in the previous chapter. Then, thankfully, you've been set free from that cursed web! Now you have a responsibility to stay out of the web. As good soldiers of Christ, we are to avoid any type of entanglement.

> *No man that warreth **entangleth** himself with the affairs of this life; that he may please him who hath chosen him to be a soldier.*
>
> *2 Timothy 2:4*

One of the laws of quantum physics is entanglement.

Quantum physics is incredibly spiritual.[67]
—Dr. Carolyn Leaf

We have been entangled with God; we are connected to Christ; we are connected to others. Satan would prefer that we were connected to him and his deadly throng, which is why he releases that strand of web, hoping to cinch us up and entangle us in his satanic realm. Do not become entangled in his trap. Stay far, far away! Entanglement denotes difficulty of escape. With every strand the enemy weaves around us, the more hopelessness we feel for any chance of escape.

> One of the things I can clearly see is that many have become so entangled they cannot move forward, and this is causing a great hopelessness in their lives.[68]
> —Charles Phillips

Those tangled in his web begin to feel the suffocating embrace of death. The more entangled we become, the harder it is to remove ourselves from his tangled web. Tangles of any kind are tricky to sort out. Take, for example, a fishing line:

> Line tangles can occur for any number of reasons including excess drag---or slack… If the fishing

67 Leaf, Dr. Carolyn. *How To Detox Your Brain Part 2.* https://www.youtube.com/watch?v=iqQoJRoZj5Q (9:47)

68 Phillips, Charles. *Elijah List: The Importance of Staying Connected to 'Next Level' People.* Aug 24, 2018. http://www.elijahlist.com/words/display_word.html?ID=20703

> line on your reel becomes tangled, **take immediate action** and free the tangles to save your line. It's possible to prevent future snarls and tangles by checking your fishing line regularly...[69]

So, too, with our lives. Christ has untangled us, yet how easy it is to fall prey again and again. We must never become slack or leave excess drag. If satan's web attaches to you, the quickest and easiest release happens when you take immediate action. Please note: it's possible to prevent future snarls by checking your line regularly. Keeping ourselves in alignment with the Word of God helps keep us free from snarls.

Receiving Christ sets us free from past entanglement, but that doesn't automatically ensure that we're no longer susceptible to satan's devious ploys and future plans. In fact, it automatically makes you his target of attack as his intention is still to pull you down from your consecrated, sacred position in Christ Jesus.

Maybe you've been part of God's family for some time. Maybe you've been passionately and completely in love with your Father; but, like King David, a fiery dart has pierced your soul, pulling you down from your consecrated and sacred position, destroying your spirit-to-spirit communication, causing hopelessness. Have you been unable to call out for help? Has the web immobilized you? Is the enemy

69 Gaston, Charlie. *How to untangle a fishing line.* https://www.trails.com/how_40966_untangle-fishing-line.html

wrapping more strands around you gaining more and more control? Or have you already been stung again by death's sting? Are you, as God's child, snagged and entangled in the web of sin?

> Do not permit the snake to write chapters in your life. You have two options in moments when the snake hisses imaginations and lofty opinions in the garden. You can make it His story, or you can keep it as history, and go on from faith to faith and glory to glory with Christ.[70]
>
> —Dawn Hill

The Apostle Paul gave us tactical keys to overcoming the antics of the enemy. Paul's command to put on the whole armour of God was given to the church—God's children. Whether we are newborn babes in Christ or mature sons, the armour of God is necessary to withstand deceitful methods of the demonic. We must intentionally dress ourselves for the war in order to quench, or extinguish, the fiery dart. Make sure you put on your armor! Above all, pick up your shield of faith! The enemy's darts are unable to penetrate your faith-shield!

70 Hill, Dawn. *Elijah List: I Hear Him Saying 'Get the Snake Out of the Garden and Make It History!'* Dec 10, 2017 http://www.elijahlist.com/words/display_word.html?ID=19317

We must intentionally dress ourselves for the war.

> I am not naive enough to believe that we do not have to engage in spiritual warfare. We must simply understand that the enemy does not have permission to set the atmosphere in the garden—which is us. When we read about the garden in Genesis, our focus tends to shift onto the fall, and we forget what was intended from the beginning. We magnify the serpent while diminishing intimacy with God. The devil needs to be addressed, and once he is addressed he needs to be removed swiftly and with the authority given to us by Christ.[71]
>
> —Dawn Hill

The enemy has been *rendered entirely useless*, disarmed by the all-powerful Christ with little left but a mouth! The "fiery dart" is the only weapon he has left and he is continually using it! With a verbiage of venom, satan is constantly shooting thoughts or suggestions into our souls and causing our minds to become a battlefield.

71 Hill, Dawn. *Elijah List: I Hear Him Saying 'Get the Snake Out of the Garden and Make It History!'* Dec 10, 2017. http://www.elijahlist.com/words/display_word.html?ID=19317

> ...the enemy will try to make your life all about him. He wants to be enthroned, and when we remain in that victim mentality instead of being more than an overcomer through Jesus Christ, we oblige him in his pursuit of exaltation without realizing it. When we entertain his notions and accusations, we consider eating from a tree that is forbidden, and we turn the garden into a battlefield.[72]
>
> —Dawn Hill

Victim mentality is characterized by negativity and always blames someone or something else for all the ills and misfortunes of life. It causes people to believe that life is out of their control. They believe that life is out to deliberately harm them. Even worse, they believe that because they've been hurt and traumatized, they're no longer responsible to press in and touch God at the heart level.

> Victim mentality isn't somebody that says I am hurt. Victim mentality says, I'm hurt and therefore I'm not responsible to rise up and touch God because I've been hurt ... I am no longer responsible for My spirit communing with God.[73]
>
> —Mike Bickle

72 Hill, Dawn. *Elijah List: I Hear Him Saying 'Get the Snake Out of the Garden and Make It History!'* Dec 10, 2017. http://www.elijahlist.com/words/display_word.html?ID=19317

73 Bickle, Mike. *Cultivating a Fiery Spirit.* CD Series

> The Kingdom mentality: we acknowledge our bruises and our hurts. But beloved, … nobody and no trauma relieves you of the God-given ability to touch God and the God-given responsibility. …Don't give up on your privilege to touch God because you've been hurt. That's your only way out of it.[74]
>
> —Mike Bickle

> **Sin is voluntary, trauma is involuntary**. …But unfortunately, it looks the same. And this is why we have to forgive. Forgiveness is absolutely essential. … Forgiveness is massive in terms of how we function.[75]
>
> —Dr. Carolyn Leaf

The enemy has definitely victimized all of us at some point, and he deliberately intends to harm us. We've all been victims, but we cannot afford to harbour a victim mentality. We have a responsibility to deal with the enemy's victimization. It's not out of our control. Jesus specifically said that He gives us power to tread on serpents and scorpions (spiders). You have the ability to trample on and crush the antics of the enemy.

> You're not helpless. You're not some victim of genetic, psychic, environmental determinism. God gave us

74 Bickle, Mike. *Cultivating a Fiery Spirit.* CD Series

75 Leaf, Dr. Carolyn. *How To Detox Your Brain Part 2.* https://www.youtube.com/watch?v=iqQoJRoZj5Q (16:07)

> power over all the power of the enemy. Sometimes you have to walk on some snakes to get where you're going. I've got some snake boots.[76]
>
> —Mark Hankins

Get your snake boots on! It's time to do some stomping! Get up and move toward God as an act of your will. The Apostle Paul gave us tactical keys to overcoming the antics of the enemy. He wrote to the church at Corinth, delivering a very important command.

> *Casting down imaginations, and every high thing that exalteth itself against the knowledge of God, and bringing into captivity every thought to the obedience of Christ;*
>
> *2 Corinthians 10:5*

Notice that this is an imperative sentence. An imperative sentence is a direct command. It begins with a verb and has no subject noun. This means that YOU are the understood subject! YOU are the one who has to do the action. In other words, YOU must "…capture every thought to make it obedient to Christ" (2 Corinthians 10:5, CEB). This is the only way to deal with a fiery dart that has pierced your mind.

> When God challenges us to bring all thoughts into captivity … He wouldn't ask us to do something that

76 Mark Hankins Ministries, CD Series. www.markhankins.org

> He didn't design us able to do. What we find from brain science is that your brain is actually designed to bring all thoughts into captivity.[77]
>
> —Dr. Carolyn Leaf

Finish off the thought rather than have the thought finish off you!

You are not to let that thought remain. Allowing thoughts of depression, lust, perversion, suicide, fear, hate, … (the list is seemingly endless) … to run rampant through your head results in a seemingly endless struggle. Struggling only results in more entanglement. Entertaining his thoughts produces struggle. Never play tug-of-war with the enemy's enticing suggestions. Wrestling with his ideas is not beneficial; in fact, it could be lethal.

> Struggling only furthers its entanglement until the spider arrives, at which point the insect is finished off with a bite.[78]

Instead, why not finish off the thought rather than have the thought finish off you! You're in a battle of epic proportion. Unlike any battle you could comprehend, it is fierce

77 Leaf, Dr. Carolyn. *How To Detox Your Brain Part 2.* https://www.youtube.com/watch?v=iqQoJRoZj5Q (2:27)

78 Hawkes, Alison. *Here We Go A-Spidering.* https://baynature.org/article/spiders/

and deadly serious. Battle denotes the possibility of being captured. The Apostle Paul gave us warning:

> *See to it that no one takes you captive through philosophy and empty* ***deception****...*
>
> *Colossians 2:8 (NASB)*

Empty deception has the ability to take us captive, but ... we are anointed to overcome!

> Anointed to Untangle —
>
> The Apostle Paul was a "Next Level Person" who was able to navigate this life successfully, while bringing the Kingdom of God in force everywhere he went. ..."Next Level People" are the warriors who refuse to be entangled or focused on things of this life. They are the ones who have set the Kingdom of God before them and are running passionately into it. They possess an anointing to speak with authority and untangle those who are trapped in the confusion and affairs of this life.[79]
>
> —Charles Phillips

I love the phrase *anointed to untangle*. We are powerful and capable. We have the anointing and the ability to sever

79 Phillips, Charles. *Elijah List: The Importance of Staying Connected to 'Next Level' People*. Aug 24, 2018. http://www.elijahlist.com/words/display_word.html?ID=20703

ourselves from the web that the enemy twisted and weaved around us. And … we have the anointing to help others who are trapped.

9. DEMOLISH THE THREAD

You are not to be the captive, but the captor. You must capture every thought that is not a God-thought or thought from Christ. There's a way to cut the web-strand intended to cinch you up. There's a way to extinguish the fiery dart that has embedded itself in your soul. Here it is: bring every unregenerate thought into captivity! This is of utmost importance. In fact, it will save your life! Your warfare weapons are not carnal, because you aren't fighting flesh and blood. That means you can't fight satan with sticks and clubs, or guns and knives. Your weapons don't come from the physical realm. They don't even make sense to our natural minds—but they are mighty!

(For the weapons of our warfare are not carnal, but mighty through God to the pulling down of strong holds;)
2 Corinthians 10:4

Pulling down of strongholds? Where are these strongholds?

> We develop a stronghold in our thought patterns. Strongholds are built by believing a series of lies that we stack like bricks around our mind. It is an actual structure and not the person. You cannot argue or reason with the brick wall and you cannot argue or reason with a stronghold in a person's mind, but You can shine a light into it.[80]
>
> —Ken & Jeanne Harrington

> ...lies are only powerful if you believe them.[81]
>
> —Blake Healy

Bring every unregenerate thought into captivity!

How many strongholds have been built in your head because you've believed the lies of satan? It's time to break some chains, crush some strongholds, destroy some walls, and defeat the enemy! What are the weapons that will pull down the stronghold in your head? Let's put the two verses in their proper order.

80 Harrington, Ken and Jeanne. *From Curses to Blessings*, Destiny Image Publishers, Inc. Shippensburg, PA. 2011. Pg 147.

81 Healy, Blake. *The Veil.* Charisma House, Charisma Media/Charisma House Book Group, Lake Mary, FL. 2018. Pg 35.

> *(For the weapons of our warfare are not carnal, but mighty through God to the pulling down of strong holds;)* ***Casting down imaginations****, and every high thing that exalteth itself against the knowledge of God, and bringing into captivity every thought to the obedience of Christ;*
>
> *2 Corinthians 10:4–5*

Weapon #1: *Cast down imaginations*: This literally means to demolish and destroy imaginations, thoughts, and attitudes that are contrary to God's thoughts and commands. Every idea, notion, or contemplation of sin must be "brought into captivity," forced into compliance or submission to alternatively hearken to the commands of Christ. 2 Corinthians 10:6 uses strong verbiage and tells us to have a "...readiness to revenge all disobedience..." You must be ready to retaliate and punish every thought of disobedience. You need to protect your mind.

> Don't give up on your God-given ability to touch God just because you are in a season of sin or trauma. Stand up and move into God![82]
>
> —Mike Bickle

Weapon #2: *Renew your mind*: Renewing means to renovate and restore.

82 Bickle, Mike. *Cultivating a Fiery Spirit.* CD Series

...be ye transformed by the renewing of your mind...
Romans 12:2

For to be carnally minded is death; but to be spiritually minded is life and peace.
Romans 8:6

You have been given the "mind of Christ" (1 Corinthians 2:16), and you must protect your mind. Proverbs 4:23 tells us to guard our hearts with all diligence because every issue of life flows out of it. *Heart* in this verse is a Hebrew word that refers to feelings, will, and intellect. We're told to guard and preserve our feelings (emotions), our will (desires and intentions), and our intellect (reasoning and judgment). This is our warfare—guarding our souls! This is necessary because thoughts produce actions.

> Thoughts precede action. We know from brain science that you can't say or do without a root and the root is the thoughts. Thoughts are very powerful things. They are very powerful, they are very physical and they are very changeable. ...Thoughts are accessible and they are designed to be re-designed.[83]
>
> —Dr. Carolyn Leaf

83 Leaf, Dr. Carolyn. *How To Detox Your Brain Part 2.* https://www.youtube.com/watch?v=iqQoJRoZj5Q (3:45)

The war is in your head. Carnal, fleshly thoughts lead to death! These aren't just impotent contemplations. They're venomous verbiage meant to penetrate your soul and lead you down a deadly path!

> Unhealthy thoughts: the proteins fall incorrectly and build these toxic looking thoughts. These are real things, they occupy mental real estate. Now here's the wonderful thing, we can get rid of these things. This is not who you are, this is who you have become.[84]
>
> —Dr. Carolyn Leaf

> Whatever you are thinking about is having this very powerful impact on your spiritual development and on your physical development and feeding back into your mind. So if you stay in that zone, you're a mess—physically and mentally.[85]
>
> —Dr. Carolyn Leaf

> …an unregenerate mind is a horrible weapon that can be used against us, causing us to reject the very answer we need.[86]
>
> —Bill Johnson

84 Leaf, Dr. Carolyn. *How To Detox Your Brain Part 2.* https://www.youtube.com/watch?v=iqQoJRoZj5Q (14:10)

85 Leaf, Dr. Carolyn. *How To Detox Your Brain Part 2.* https://www.youtube.com/watch?v=iqQoJRoZj5Q (8:20)

86 Johnson, Bill. *The War in Your Head.* Destiny Image Publishers, Inc. Shippensburg, PA. 2014. Pg 36.

We must constantly renew our minds—renovating and restoring the neural pathways of being "spiritually minded." King David learned this the hard way, and yet:

> David gave a good example to us when he commanded his emotions and his mind to come into line with the truth about God. He wrote in Psalm 103:1-2 *Bless the Lord, O my soul; and all that is within me, bless His holy name! Bless the Lord, O my soul, and forget not all His benefits...* We can yank our minds and emotions back into line with reality.[87]
>
> —Bill Johnson

Yank your mind back into line by:

Weapon #3: *Change your affections*: change what you focus on.

> *Set your affection on things above, not on things on the earth.*
>
> *Colossians 3:2*

Set your affection is the Greek word [phroneo] which means: to exercise the mind, entertain a sentiment, interest oneself in.[88] Exercise is an activity that requires effort.

87 Johnson, Bill. *The War in Your Head.* Destiny Image Publishers, Inc. Shippensburg, PA. 2014. Pg 39.

88 Staggs, Brandon. SwordSearcher, *Interlinear KJV with Strong's Greek & Hebrew Lexicon.* iPhone app. Apple App Store. Vers. 3.4. Brandon Staggs, 1999.

What kind of mind-movies are you watching? Your thoughts should serve you rather than sabotage you. It will require effort to change the channel, and it will require consistency to keep the channel changed.

> *From now on, brothers and sisters … focus your thoughts on these things: all that is true, all that is holy, all that is just, all that is pure, all that is lovely, and all that is worthy of praise.*
>
> *Philippians 4:8 (CEB)*

Take every wicked, alluring, devious thought captive and focus on a different mind-movie—the true, the holy, the pure. Exercise increases strength and endurance. With each exercise, you gain muscle. Each victory empowers you for the next.

> …after a time the silk will lose its stickiness and thus become inefficient at capturing prey.[89]

As you exercise your soul, the threaded dart hurled at you will soon lose its stickiness. That dart then becomes inefficient at enticing you.

> Temptation can only occur when you want something. You cannot tempt me with what I do not want.[90]
>
> —Bishop TD Jakes

89 Wikipedia, s.v. "Spider web." https://en.wikipedia.org/wiki/Spider_web

90 Jakes, Bishop TD. *Denial Produces Discipline-40 Days,* https://www.youtube.com/watch?v=UfzHs2z17Yc&t=1242s

Remember: The dart—the question, the thought, the idea—is not the sin, but a means of enticing you to sin. Many feel condemned and defeated (and sinful) whenever the dart (thought or temptation) arrives. Again, this is just another ploy of the enemy as he makes us question our salvation, our holiness, and … our sanity.

> Satan is always raising questions, Jesus is always raising the Word.[91]
>
> —Jentezen Franklin

This is spiritual warfare! What we need to do—immediately, if not sooner—is combat the thoughts that are exalting themselves and bring them into obedience, the obedience of Christ's commands, not the enemy's suggestions.

> So, don't prolong your inevitable battles, use the foundational truth in the word of God - the weapons of your warfare - and keep the enemy on his toes! We are more than conquerors in Christ Jesus![92]
>
> —James Goll

91 Franklin, Jentezen. *Spirit of Python: Snake Eggs in Your Head.* https://www.youtube.com/watch?v=HW8JGWAd0N0 (24:28)

92 Goll, James. *Elijah List: 7 Ways to Shorten Your Seasons of Struggle.* Encounters Network, The Elijah List, Apr 15, 2018. http://elijahlist.com/words/display_word.html?ID=20003

Be clearheaded. Keep alert. Your accuser, the devil, is on the prowl ... seeking someone to devour.
1 Peter 5:8 (CEB)

Satan is the father of lies (John 8:44). Anytime you hear a lie in your head, it's the enemy speaking and you need to recognize that. Here's a simple test for determining who's speaking to you: God always calls you by your destiny and covenant, but the enemy always calls you by your issues! Don't get wrapped up in the lies of the deceiver. If all you hear in your head are the constant issues and problems of your life, such as your *flawed* character, your *poor* qualities, your *in*-abilities, your *horrid* circumstances, then without a doubt it's the venomous whispers of a hateful foe. All the adjectives are wrong! Like the spider, satan's nutrition comes from consuming his prey. His only strength comes from ... you! Your agreement with his suggestions empowers the one who has been disempowered. Crush his deception with a God-thought! Combat his lies with pure truth! Fill your mind with God's realities! Meditate on His Word! Truth always prevails! Demolish the thread of his web with the truth of Christ! Cut the thread that cinches you to his deceptions and contradictions. Keep your mind free from the redundant, circuitous ramblings of a compulsive liar. Satan's tactics never change. When the devil attacks—intensify Jesus!

I just can't stand lies and I'm tired of watching the body of Christ be in fear over nothing... every day is

> another opportunity to destroy hell… I can't afford to think with fear. I can't afford to think with thoughts that aren't in God's mind.[93]
>
> —Todd White

Keep your mind free from the redundant, circuitous ramblings of a compulsive liar.

It's possible to renew your mind! God wouldn't have given us the command if it was an impossibility! If you are having trouble with renewing your mind, simply ask God for help. Here's a simple prayer: Jesus, I ask you to cleanse my mind, renew my mind, transform me, and set me free! Thank you, Jesus!

> If you see the reality and magnitude of what Jesus really did, the only option is complete surrender; complete abandonment to who [you are] so that [you] can absolutely, 100% positively go after Him—with 100% of [you] … soul included!
>
> This is a life that is completely abandoned, to where the mindset that you carried—victim mindset, guilty, ashamed, condemned, regret mindset—gets to be

93 White, Todd. *Unstoppable with Jesus*. https://www.youtube.com/watch?v=hfX9lTLTeek (10:10)

transformed, because guilt and sin … all this stuff, it's all junk from an old life.[94]

—Todd White

Summing it all up, friends, I'd say you'll do best by filling your minds and meditating on things true, noble, reputable, authentic, compelling, gracious—the best, not the worst; the beautiful, not the ugly; things to praise, not things to curse. Put into practice what you learned from me, what you heard and saw and realized. Do that, and God, who makes everything work together, will work you into his most excellent harmonies.

Philippians 4:8 (MSG)

94 White, Todd. *When the Devil Attacks—Intensify Jesus.* https://www.youtube.com/watch?v=hfX9lTLTeek (20:00)

10.
COLD-BLOODED

By now, you should have gained revelation that the web is really *very* delicate and fragile. Understanding your empowerment as God's child—and satan's disempowerment as God's adversary—is vital! (Even the statement that satan is God's adversary is quite comical and ludicrous.) Satan against God? That's not even a battle! There's no comparison between the strength of the two forces. Satan falls before the presence and power of God so quickly that one cannot even discern that he has ever been there. And, satan against you? The odds are just as unbalanced. One plus God equals a majority!

If there's anything we *do* know about our foe, it's that he is persistent. But there's something else you *should* know. Unlike you, both snakes and spiders are cold-blooded, limiting them. So, a snake or spider…

> ...being cold-blooded, is limited in its ability to endure, to keep going. Therefore, you can outlast it.[95]
>
> —Jonathan Cahn

If serpents and spiders are cold-blooded, then in some way, so is evil.

> Evil is cold-blooded. What that means is this: Though evil may have its day, its victories, its time to move and strike—it remains cold-blooded. Therefore, it can never endure. No matter how powerful the evil may appear, no matter how triumphant and unstoppable it may seem, it cannot last. ... And so the power of evil is only for the short-term and the momentary. Its days are always numbered. And in the long run, it always fails.[96]
>
> —Jonathan Cahn

In truth, that freaky apparatus with too many legs creeping across your floor is much more scared of you than you are of it.[97]

95 Cahn, Jonathan. *The Book of Mysteries.* (Lake Mary, FL: FrontLine, 2016.), Pg. 10. Used by permission

96 Cahn, Jonathan. *The Book of Mysteries.* (Lake Mary, FL: FrontLine, 2016.), Pg. 10. Used by permission

97 *Death From Snake Or Spider Bite Is Extremely Rare.* https://knowledgenuts.com/2014/05/06/death-from-snake-or-spider-bite-is-extremely-rare/

In truth, satan is absolutely terrified of YOU! You can outlast and out-power him. You are stronger and more durable than him. He is NOT triumphant, and he is most certainly stoppable. One day we will see him for who he really is! One day we will see how absolutely defeated, paralyzed, and truly disarmed he really is. The Bible tells us our reaction on this day.

> *...people will stare and muse: "Can this be the one who terrorized earth and its kingdoms ... shut up his prisoners to a living death?"*
>
> *Isaiah 14:16–17 (MSG)*

How important it is that we get revelation of this sooner rather than later! May you never again be held captive by his web, held prisoner to a living death. He could never take you on without first enveloping you in his sticky, repulsive, reprehensible trap and holding you as prisoner. Don't forget: Jesus has picked up that scorpion (spider) and plucked the stinger right out of Him!

> *O death, where is thy sting?*
>
> *1 Corinthians 15:55a*

> The devil and his minions are filled with terror. Although they are not omniscient, omnipotent or omni-anything, they do know that their time is short, and this knowledge increases their wrath. They are

trying to wreak as much carnage as possible before the final curtain goes down. This can help us as soldiers in God's army. We can adopt an attitude that says, "Satan, you may have inflicted some wounds on me, but you do not have the final word. I've seen the end of the book, and I know you will lose."

Every skirmish has the same ultimate outcome—victory in Jesus! The last words of Jesus on the Cross must be the last words in our mouth and heart, "It is finished!"[98]

—James Goll

98 Goll, James. *Elijah List: 7 Ways to Shorten Your Seasons of Struggle.* Encounters Network, The Elijah List, Apr 15, 2018. http://elijahlist.com/words/display_word.html?ID=20003 Apr 15, 2018

11. A CHILD'S FINGER

Sons and daughters of God have amazing privileges and benefits. You've been surrounded with favour, sheltered in His love, and promised victory. You're far more powerful than you know! Jesus has given you an incredible amount of power and authority—in fact, He has shared His power with you because you have become a joint-heir with Christ.

> *...we are the children of God: And if children, then heirs; heirs of God, and joint-heirs with Christ...*
>
> *Romans 8:16–17*

He proved His dominance over every principality and power, and victoriously declared:

> *...**All** power is given unto me in heaven and in earth.*
>
> *Matthew 28:18*

Jesus gave His life for us, so what would He withhold from us? Absolutely nothing! Therefore, He's also given you His power. He sovereignly empowered you against a relentless foe. In Mark's gospel, Jesus gathers His twelve disciples together and confers an incredible capability on them.

> *After Jesus called the twelve together* ***he gave them power and authority*** *over* ***all*** *demons and to cure diseases.*
>
> *Luke 9:1 (NET)*

You are far more powerful than you know!

How many demons did they have power over? All. All means: each one of, every single one of.[99] Before sending His disciples into the world without physically accompanying them, Jesus gave them power and authority over the totality of the demonic hordes. Not one adversary had more power than His disciples. Many of God's children think this power was for His original twelve followers only, so let's keep reading as Jesus appoints seventy others. The seventy went on their mission and returned "with joy." To their great delight, they found out that devils were subject to them.

99 *New Oxford American Dictionary.* Oxford: Oxford University Press, 2010.

After these things the Lord appointed seventy others also…

Luke 10:1 (NKJV)

And the seventy returned again with joy, saying, Lord, even the devils are subject unto us through thy name.

Luke 10:17

Jesus gave His disciples power and authority over the totality of the demonic hordes.

You can feel the surprise and delight in their statement as they realized that devils were "subject" to them. The devils were caused to be compliant to the commands of Christ's followers. Every devil was in subordination. Every devil now had a lower-ranking position, forced into a subservient state of submission—yielding, compliant, deferential obedience to Christ's followers.

The story found in Luke 10 takes us back to the morning of my dream when God spoke into my heart: *Just like I watched Satan fall like lightning from heaven, he fell before you so quickly that you could hardly even discern it was him. He fell before you because you're covered with the blood, and nothing shall by any means harm you.*

The devils were caused to be compliant to the commands of Christ's followers.

Let's read the passage in Luke 10 and see the power delegated to them—and to us!

> *And he said unto them, I beheld Satan as lightning fall from heaven.* ***Behold, I give unto you power to tread on serpents and scorpions, and over all the power of the enemy:*** *and nothing shall by any means hurt you.*
>
> *Luke 10:18–19*

The power of redeemed man is beyond our comprehension.

The *power* Jesus gave to us is the Greek word [exousia] and is different from the word used for power of the enemy. [Exousia] means: the sense of ability, force, capacity, competency, freedom, power, right, strength.[100] Another word in [exousia]'s long list of meanings is the word: superhuman.[101] The exceptional power and ability to influence and direct the behaviour of devils does not come from our own human

100 Staggs, Brandon. SwordSearcher, *Interlinear KJV with Strong's Greek & Hebrew Lexicon.* iPhone app. Apple App Store. Vers. 3.4. Brandon Staggs, 1999.

101 Staggs, Brandon. SwordSearcher, *Interlinear KJV with Strong's Greek & Hebrew Lexicon.* iPhone app. Apple App Store. Vers. 3.4. Brandon Staggs, 1999.

abilities. We've been given power to trample and crush serpents and scorpions (spiders)—devils and demons. This power comes from the all-powerful Spirit of our living Lord.

> *... "Not by might nor by power, but by My Spirit," says the Lord of hosts.*
>
> *Zechariah 4:6 (NKJV)*

The weakness of fallen man is feeble and frail. It's weakness in its lowest form. But the power of redeemed man is beyond our comprehension. The redeemed of the Lord have been endued with a *superhuman* power—the power of Jesus Christ, a power greater than *any* power or principality. Too many people assume this power was reserved for the twelve or the seventy. Let's read the last recorded words of Jesus in the book of Mark. Jesus again commissions His followers and reminds us of our ability-of-power and position-of-authority that supersede any ability or control the devil may have. These final words were given just moments prior to Him ascending into heaven.

> *...these signs shall follow* ***them that believe****; In my name shall they* ***cast out devils****; they shall speak with new tongues; They shall* ***take up serpents****; and if they* ***drink any deadly thing****, it shall not hurt them; they shall lay hands on the sick, and they shall recover.*
>
> *Mark 16:17–18*

Believe means: *have faith*. My friend, if you have chosen Christ as your Saviour, you are far more powerful than any demon or devil. You have been placed in a position of power that is more powerful than every force of darkness. You have been given great authority! Even the weakest, newest baby born into the Kingdom of God has greater power than satan and his cohorts.

> *Out of the mouth of babes and sucklings hast thou ordained strength* ***because of*** *thine enemies, that thou mightest still the enemy and the avenger.*
>
> *Psalm 8:2*

King David sang a song in Psalm 8 that has great prophetic implications, and conveys the power of God's children. God *ordained* strength in the mouth of his children—he even goes as far as saying *babes* (infants) and *sucklings* (those still drinking milk). *Ordain* means: to confer holy orders on. God conferred strength on your mouth *because* you have an enemy. You have been given a mouth [peh]: the mouth, (particularly speech.)[102] You must speak!

> Some find spiders and their hairy legs terrifying. **But research has shown those hairs are so sensitive they can detect human speech from several metres**

102 Staggs, Brandon. SwordSearcher, *Interlinear KJV with Strong's Greek & Hebrew Lexicon.* iPhone app. Apple App Store. Vers. 3.4. Brandon Staggs, 1999.

> **away**... Surprisingly, we found that they possess an acute sense of hearing... They can hear sounds at distances much farther away than previously thought, even though they lack ears with the eardrums typical of most animals with long-distance hearing.[103]

Satan definitely hears you! He has an acute ability to hear human speech, even from long distances away. And believe me, he wishes that he didn't. The mouths of God's babies have a dominant, influential, controlling strength **because of** their enemies. No matter how old you are in the Kingdom of God, your mouth has the ability to subdue the devil. King David tells us that our mouths are to still the enemy [oyeb]: (hating adversary)[104] and the avenger [naqam]: (to grudge).[105] The devil is a hating adversary with a grudge. Satan's rage knows no bounds! He hates you with a powerful vengeance, hosting a deep-seated grudge against you because of the powerful love-redemption God implemented on your behalf. Therefore, God decided that His children needed a defense against this hateful adversary. Your mouth has the ability to *still* the enemy and the avenger. In this verse, *still*

103 The Guardian (International Edition). *Spiders don't have ears—but they can still hear you coming.* https://www.theguardian.com/science/2016/oct/13/spiders-dont-have-ears-but-they-can-still-hear-you-coming

104 Staggs, Brandon. SwordSearcher, *Interlinear KJV with Strong's Greek & Hebrew Lexicon.* iPhone app. Apple App Store. Vers. 3.4. Brandon Staggs, 1999.

105 Staggs, Brandon. SwordSearcher, *Interlinear KJV with Strong's Greek & Hebrew Lexicon.* iPhone app. Apple App Store. Vers. 3.4. Brandon Staggs, 1999.

is used as a verb. When used as a verb, still means: to make or become still, quieten.[106] Again, satan's weapon against us is the words he releases into our minds. But you have the ability to silence the liar.

The mouths of God's babies have a dominant, influential, controlling strength.

> We must overcome the venom and poisonous effects of poor perception. The devil has been extremely active attempting to confuse and sidetrack the Saints, endeavoring to keep them away from their true identity … It is important that we discover how to silence every voice that is contrary to his voice.[107]
>
> —Bobby Conner

Since you have an enemy, God gave you a mouth. And with your mouth you have the ability to silence satan. This is even better than having to extinguish the dart's fire once it has penetrated your soul. Wow! YOU have the ability to silence the bitter words, deceptive lies, cruel jabs, and seductive suggestions of his mouth before they are even released.

106 *New Oxford American Dictionary.* Oxford: Oxford University Press, 2010.
107 Conner, Bobby. *Shepherd's Rod Volume 23: SONSHIP – SHIFTING FROM SERVANT TO SON…DISCOVERING YOU ARE HEIR TO THE KINGDOM.* Distributed by: Eagle's View Ministries — A division of Bobby Conner, Demonstration of God's Power Ministries, Bullard, TX. Pg 16, 29.

Your praises still the enemy! Your praises cause him to be silenced! Even the weakest member of God's family is more powerful than *every* entity of darkness. It's time that you speak back!

You have the ability to silence the liar.

Never run at your giant with your mouth closed.[108]
—Mark Hankins

Staying silent will cause you to lose by default! Satan's tongue is a weapon, but your tongue is a weapon also. Your lips are blood-covered and blood-bought. You have the ability, the ammunition, the power, and the authority to address the enemy.

> ...when we address the serpent—and we place him under our feet as the Body of Christ—we send him slithering...[109]
>
> —Dawn Hill

The words of God are a force to be reckoned with, and with His words in your mouth, so are YOU! Filled with Holy Spirit, covered with armour, equipped with faith, speak the

108 Mark Hankin Ministries, CD Series. www.markhankins.org

109 Hill, Dawn, *Elijah List: I Hear Him Saying 'Get the Snake Out of the Garden and Make It History!'* Dec 10, 2017. http://www.elijahlist.com/words/display_word.html?ID=19317

Word of God into your situation. You aren't wrestling with flesh and blood. The next time satan's web springs at you in attack, lift up your voice, declare God's truth, and silence the voice of satan. Without God's Word, we would be unable to withstand the battle, much less fight it. God's Word in your mouth is your most powerful weapon.

> ...Reinhard Bonnke said the Lord told him, My Word in your mouth is just as powerful as My Word in My mouth.[110]
>
> —Mark Hankins

> And you are here to give the devil a bad day. Every day of your life you are to give the devil a bad day.[111]
>
> —Todd White

In the thick of battle, whether you're feeling strong and fearless or weak and vulnerable, take up the weapon of praise and put His words in your mouth. Satan is persistent, but the father of lies cannot withstand your shouted praise or whispered truths. The real truth is that YOU are satan's enemy! Use pure truth to combat his lies. Your words contain unprecedented, immeasurable power that breaks chains,

110 Hankins, Mark. *Never Run at the Devil with Your Mouth Shut.* https://www.cfaith.com/index.php/blog/23-articles/victory/19139-never-run-at-the-devil-with-your-mouth-shut

111 White, Todd. *Unstoppable with Jesus.* https://www.youtube.com/watch?v=_cKEotvZ04I&t=429s (9:17)

crushes strongholds, destroys walls, and defeats armies. It's time to smash down warped philosophies, tear down barriers, demolish corrupt communications, and **erect the truth**.

> As you know, some of these giants can be persistent. Speaking the Word of God releases God's power to win in each conflict. Winning the war of words is necessary to win the fight of faith. …Never let the devil have the last word.[112]
>
> —Mark Hankins

You are anointed with the Spirit of the Sovereign Lord. You have been equipped with an anointing that destroys every yoke of the devil. You are anointed to untangle and destroy the deceits of satan. The fiery arrows shot at you are his last-ditch attempts to lure you into sin, harass, and tyrannize you. It's his feeble attempt to domineer someone who has been given dominion. You have been given power and authority over **every** devil, over every addiction, over every perversion, over every oppression, and over every lie that is meant to seduce you into his demonic trap. You have been given the ability to tread on serpents and scorpions.

With revelation of your empowerment as God's child and satan's disempowerment as God's adversary, you now know that the fatal web is also very delicate and fragile. A web with

112 Hankins, Mark. *Never Run at the Devil with Your Mouth Shut.* https://www.cfaith.com/index.php/blog/23-articles/victory/19139-never-run-at-the-devil-with-your-mouth-shut

the tensile strength of steel is able to be quickly swept away to nothingness with a child's finger—God's child, YOU!

So, **is the web fatal or fragile?** It all depends on who's going through it. It all depends on … you. Will you sweep it away, or remain tangled in its grip? Jesus has supplied the antivenom and given you power to sweep away the web that has held you captive for so long. You thought it was strong, powerful, and lethal, but in reality, it's fragile, delicate, and easily broken.

That's it! Go ahead! Take your little finger and swipe away all the tattered, tangled webs that have held you captive for so long. You, my friend, have been created to be glorious and victorious! It's time to prosper in your soul! You've been set free! Your soul has escaped the snare of the fowler!

The snare is broken, and we have escaped.
Psalm 124:7b (NKJV)

Blessed be the Lord, who hath not given us as a prey to their teeth.

Psalm 124:6

About the Author

Dr. Wendy Varga ministers at Portal of Glory Christian Ministries International, which was founded by her parents, Moses and Rosemary Sabo, in Edmonton, Alberta, Canada. A significant part of Portal of Glory's vision is to equip God's people, preparing them to fulfill God's purpose for their lives. Wendy taught an accredited Bible school for several years, equipping others to reach their full potential. She carries a deep passion for the nations and desires to see others come into a deeper understanding of the roots of their faith.

As a fourth generation pastor, author, speaker, and songwriter, Wendy's ministry to the Church revealing the power contained in Jesus Christ and Communion's Love Feast is profoundly important. Committed to sharing intimate and deep revelation of the power of His Body and Blood, Wendy inspires others to feast on the very Source of life—Jesus Christ.

Special Acknowledgment

All glory to the One who has delivered me and did not leave me as prey in the jaws of the devourer. Jesus is so faithful to me!

Acknowledgments

Many thanks to all who have touched my life in any way. You have encouraged and empowered me to overcome. My life is enriched by so many family and friends, each unique perspective contributing to who I am today.

Special thanks to:

- My true partner in life and faith—Michael Varga: My love for you is stronger than ever. Thank you for standing by my side and encouraging me daily in my many projects. Thank you for praying for and believing in me. I will forever be grateful to you.
- My children—Jevon, Jeneca and Vincent, Jalyn, and those yet to come: You are my reward and heritage, filling my life with joy and the wonder of living. I know that you will faithfully teach your children the ways of the Lord. You have incredibly blessed my life, and you are destined for greatness.
- My parents—Moses and Rosemary Sabo: The touch of God on your life is so apparent. Your daily prayers and

encouragement are invaluable. Thank you for being so instrumental in my faith-walk and continually upholding me with your loving and tender strength. You faithfully cultivate an amazing legacy to live up to.

- My parents-in-law—Peter and Katie Varga: You so welcomed and accepted me into your family with deepest love. Your hard word and generosity were truly amazing. I so miss you!

References

Bickle, Mike. *Cultivating a Fiery Spirit.* CD Series

Biting Back. https://www.aaas.org/sites/default/files/sw-091613-bitingback.pdf

Cahn, Jonathan. *The Book of Mysteries.* (Lake Mary, FL: FrontLine, 2016.). Used by permission.

Conner, Bobby. *Shepherd's Rod Volume 23: SONSHIP – SHIFTING FROM SERVANT TO SON... DISCOVERING YOU ARE HEIR TO THE KINGDOM.* Distributed by: Eagle's View Ministries — A division of Bobby Conner, Demonstration of God's Power Ministries, Bullard, TX.

Death From Snake Or Spider Bite Is Extremely Rare. https://knowledgenuts.com/2014/05/06/death-from-snake-or-spider-bite-is-extremely-rare/

Franklin, Jentezen. *Spirit of Python: Snake Eggs in Your Head.* https://www.youtube.com/watch?v=HW8JGWAd0N0

Gaston, Charlie. *How to untangle a fishing line.* https://www.trails.com/how_40966_untangle-fishing-line.html

Goll, James. *Elijah List: 7 Ways to Shorten Your Seasons of Struggle.* Encounters Network, The Elijah List, Apr 15, 2018. http://elijahlist.com/words/display_word.html?ID=20003

Goll, James. *Elijah List: It's Time This Thing Gets Exposed.* Encounters Network, The Elijah List, Nov 29, 2017. http://www.elijahlist.com/words/display_word.html?ID=19246

Goll, James. *Elijah List: How to Overcome Satan's 4 Favorite Tactics.* Encounters Network, The Elijah List, Aug 31, 2016. http://www.elijahlist.com/words/display_word.html?ID=16560

Hankins, Mark. Mark Hankins Ministries, CD Series. www.markhankins.org

Hankins, Mark. *Never Run at the Devil with Your Mouth Shut.* https://www.cfaith.com/index.php/blog/23-articles/victory/19139-never-run-at-the-devil-with-your-mouth-shut

Harrington, Ken and Jeanne. *From Curses to Blessings*, Destiny Image Publishers, Inc. Shippensburg, PA. 2011.

Harris, Tom. *How Spiders Work.* https://animals.howstuffworks.com/arachnids/spider5.htm

Hawkes, Alison. *Here We Go A-Spidering.* https://baynature.org/article/spiders/

Healy, Blake. *The Veil.* Charisma House, Charisma Media/Charisma House Book Group, Lake Mary, FL. 2018.

Hill, Dawn. *Elijah List: I Hear Him Saying 'Get the Snake Out of the Garden and Make It History!'.* Dec 10, 2017. http://www.elijahlist.com/words/display_word.html?ID=19317

How Does Antivenom Work in Our Bodies When Injected. Quora.https://www.quora.com/How-does-anti-venom-work-in-our-bodies-when-injected

Jakes, Bishop TD. *Denial Produces Discipline-40 Days,* https://www.youtube.com/watch?v=UfzHs2z17Yc&t=1242s

Jimenez, Alberto Corsin. Spanish National Research Council, *Spider web anthropology's: ecologies, infrastructures, entanglement's,* http://digital.csic.es/

bitstream/10261/134351/1/spiderweb%20anthros_160209.pdf

Johnson, Bill. *The War in Your Head.* Destiny Image Publishers, Inc. Shippensburg, PA. 2014.

Leaf, Dr. Carolyn. *How To Detox Your Brain Part 2.* https://www.youtube.com/watch?v=iqQoJRoZj5Q

Lenhardt, Karin. *76 Interesting Facts about Snakes.* https://www.factretriever.com/snake-facts

Lehnardt, Karin. *84 Amazing Facts about Spiders.* https://www.factretriever.com/spider-facts

Milking Spiders For Their Venom. https://www.terminix.com/blog/science-nature/milking-spiders-for-their-venom/

New Oxford American Dictionary. Oxford: Oxford University Press, 2010.

Pereira, Dr. Anand & Geeta. *Antivenom: Why it's So Precious!* http://www.daijiworld.com/chan/exclusiveDisplay.aspx?articlesID=2609

Phillips, Charles. *Elijah List: The Importance of Staying Connected to 'Next Level' People.* Aug 24,

2018. http://www.elijahlist.com/words/display_word.html?ID=20703

Phillips, Trish. *More Animal Symbolism.* http://www.pure-spirit.com/more-animal-symbolism/664-spider-symbolism

Piper, John. *Desiring God.* https://www.desiringgod.org/messages/the-son-of-man-must-be-lifted-up-like-the-serpent

Puiu, Tibi. *Antivenom: how it's made and why it's so precious.* https://www.zmescience.com/other/feature-post/antivenom-made-precious/

Richman, Richard. *Do spiders have tongues?* http://www.madsci.org/posts/archives/2000-12/977577464.Gb.r.html

Science News, Unlocking The Psychology Of Snake And Spider Phobias, https://www.sciencedaily.com/releases/2008/03/080320132646.htm

Sowing Circle. Blue Letter Bible, *Interlinear Concordance.* iPhone app. Apple App Store. Vers. 2.54. Sowing Circle. 2016.

Spider Fangs Make Perfect Injection Needles. https://www.seeker.com/spider-fangs-make-perfect-injection-needles-1768601045.html

Spider vs. Scorpion Identification. https://www.orkin.com/stinging-pests/scorpions/spider-vs-scorpion-identification/

Staggs, Brandon. SwordSearcher, *Easton's Bible Dictionary.* iPhone app. Apple App Store. Vers. 3.4. Brandon Staggs, 1999.

Staggs, Brandon. SwordSearcher, *Interlinear KJV with Strong's Greek & Hebrew Lexicon.* iPhone app. Apple App Store. Vers. 3.4. Brandon Staggs, 1999.

Stockton, Nick. *The Secret History of Spider Venom's Paralytic Power.* https://www.wired.com/2015/06/secret-origin-spectacular-spider-venom/

The Guardian (International Edition). *Spiders don't have ears—but they can still hear you coming.* https://www.theguardian.com/science/2016/oct/13/spiders-dont-have-ears-but-they-can-still-hear-you-coming

Truth or Tradition? https://www.truthortradition.com/articles/why-does-the-truth-offend

Wade, Lizzie. *Here's How You Milk Snakes To Make Antivenom.* https://www.wired.com/2014/11/how-to-make-antivenum/

White, Todd. *Coming Back to Your First Love.* https://www.youtube.com/watch?v=FuFHDfbjo2M

White, Todd. *Unstoppable with Jesus.* https://www.youtube.com/watch?v=hfX9lTLTeek

White, Todd. *When Finances are Stolen.* https://www.youtube.com/watch?v=o4ZtHyJ8Cq8

White, Todd. *When the Devil Attacks—Intensify Jesus.* https://www.youtube.com/watch?v=hfX9lTLTeek

Wikipedia. "*Antivenom.*" https://en.wikipedia.org/wiki/Antivenom

Wikipedia, "*Spider web.*" https://en.wikipedia.org/wiki/Spider_web

Other Books by Wendy Varga

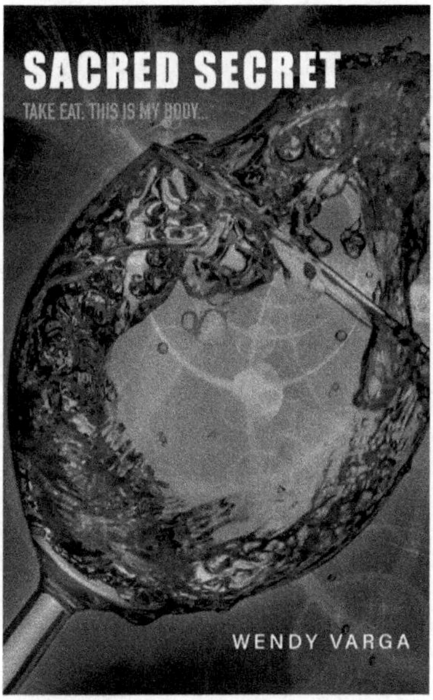

Sacred Secret: The deepest of mysteries unveiled! Discover Heaven's ultimate supremacy contained in a Meal of incredible power.

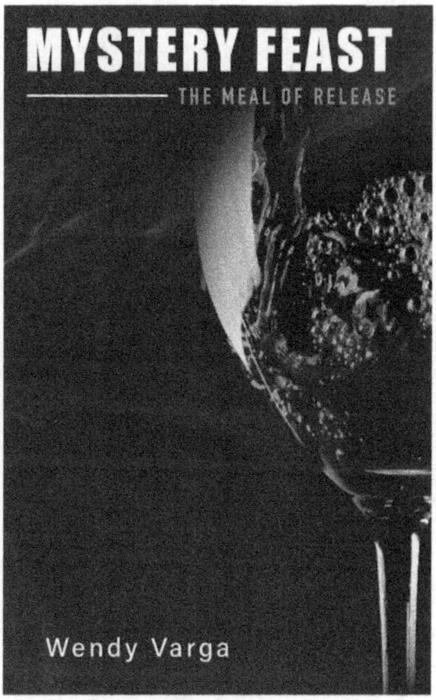

Mystery Feast: Unequalled, unrivalled power contained and served in one meal. Release Heaven's force into your deadest, darkest night.